Mel Bay Presents

IT'S A DULCIMER LIFE

Arrangements from the albums and repertoire of

Neal Hellman (www.gourd.com)

D1592089

Gail Rich, editor

Kevin Moore, computer and musical mentor

Barry Phillips, arrangements advisor and recording engineer

Paul Schraub, photographer

Special thanks to:
Joe Weed, Lin Marelick, Michael Rugg, Danny Carnahan, Coda Music Software

Dedicated to all the people who fed me, put me up
and otherwise helped me along the road for seven years of touring the United States

Visit us on the Web at www.melbay.com — E-mail us at email@melbay.com

About the author ...

Neal Hellman has been active in acoustic music since 1973. He has penned many books on the Appalachian dulcimer and has recorded numerous albums including **Oktober County** and **Dream of the Manatee.** He recently completed the soundtrack (with Joe Weed) for *Princess Furball,* an animated children's video. In 1987, Neal founded Gourd Recordings, and has produced beautiful albums including *Simple Gifts, A Victorian Christmas, Tender Shepherd, The World Turned Upside Down* and *The Fairie Round.* He lives and works in Central California with his mate and co-worker Gail, son Shiloh, and companion felines Caitlin Rose and Kalai. Neal is an avid student of history and current events and remarked on the fall of the Iron Curtain, "After all, people just want to shop."

Each dulcimer pictured in this book is more than part of my collection —
each is a dear friend, with special qualities all its own:
sound coloring, texture and personality.

It's a Dulcimer Life is set in Palatino, Petrucci and Medici Script,
using Coda Finale 2.6.3, Aldus Pagemaker 4.2 and Microsoft Word 5.0.

❤ Table of Contents ❤

❤ ❤ ❤ ❤

ABOUT THE TAPE

All the arrangements in the book are on the tape in the same order as the **Index by Songs** above.

Due to timing limitations, however, I sometimes do not observe the repeats indicated in the music. For example, in *Lauda di Maria Maddelenna,* I only play one "A" part, though you can see the music instructs you to play it twice. The same is true for *Hewlett*. On other compositions, such as *El Tutu,* I've followed the music as written.

Don't be confused if you occasionally hear me play a hammer where the music indicates a pull, or some other such variation on the written page. That's the very nature of performance ... and even I sometimes depart from my own arrangements. Isn't art great?

And finally, remember that this tape is simply for you to hear how the songs go. Please don't take my versions of these pieces as definitive. Make each one your own, with your own personal touches.

❤ Index by Album ❤

Notes & Hints On the Compositions

A problem with arranging for any instrument and printing it on a page is that it stays the same. It no longer has the dynamic character of a performance piece which can change with the personality of the player. Factors that would affect how one plays a tune can be many. They could range from the instruments one is playing with to the phases of the moon.

In the many years I have done workshops around this vast country of ours I have heard countless dulcimers of all shapes and sizes. Each individual dulcimer seems to have its own "sweet spot." Some sound better on the high strings while some emit a more beautiful tone when strummed near the bridge. Get to know your dulcimer — find out where your "sweet spot" is. Spend some quality time with your instrument, go out together, take your dulcimer to lunch, and become its friend.

Try to think of the following arrangements as one would view recipes from a cookbook. These arrangements are a great place to start but you, the player can add variations to the song or tune to make it your own. I placed many hammers, pulls and slides in the arrangements because they suited the style of playing that is best for me. You can alter, add or subtract any embellishments to suit your own individual way of playing. I use a flatpick for most of the compositions in this book but I'm sure one could finger pick instead. You might have to alter the arrangements a bit — by all means do so.

I use D-A-D tuning a lot in this book because that seems to be the tuning of choice in dulcimer land these days. The fact is, one can utilize any 1-5-1 tuning.

These tunes were arranged on several different dulcimers, hence the variety of different string arrangements.

Most of the following pieces were arranged on a dulcimer with just three strings (string guage: .010 - .014 - .024 Bronze Wound). For the delicate tunes with lots of embellishments, I find it easier to execute the ornamentations without the double first strings. It's just too awkward to do hammers and pulls on the double strings.

The compositions for four equidistant strings *(Durango, Picnic On the St. Croix* and *Lord Franklin)* were all arranged using the D-D-G-D tuning. This is a wonderful tuning to get chords that are just impossible to voice on the three-string dulcimer.

I also use a six-string which is a three-string with all courses doubled. This dulcimer is great for "back-up" work. I like to use a wound string and a plain string on the bass course to give that twelve string "twang".

A few of the arrangements were played on a very small box-shaped dulcimer which I tune G-D-G (string guage : .008 - .011 - .020) It's fun to play pieces like the Bach *Minuet* and the *Rondeau* by Mouret on this dulcimer because it sounds so sweet — like a little music box.

It's a wonderful thing to own a number of dulcimers because, after all, life is short and one does need variety to express oneself. I like to keep what I call my kick-around dulcimer handy so I can play it at any time.

Try listening to the tape first and attempt to play the arrangement the way I have written it down. After a while your own style will just start to happen.

Also try to sing the melody as you play and remember, play everything slowly at first till you feel comfortable with the piece. Please remember this: *it really is okay to have fun while you play the dulcimer.*

❤ ❤ ❤ ❤

A Song for Lori: A sad tune I wrote for Lori Parker of Nashville, Indiana who left this earth far too soon. Please note that it's in the key of G, though tuned D-A-D. This technique of playing in different keys and modes while tuned to the 1-5-1 tuning is explained in great detail in my *Dulcimer Chord Book* (pages 3-8). Remember you can be in any 1-5-1 tuning (C-G-C or E-B-E) and play the same fret numbers that appear in this arrangement — but the key will be different. Try different frets for the "back-up" chords.

You'll probably notice in many of my arrangements in the 1-5-1 tuning, I like the lead note of the back-up chord to be played on the bass string. For example, in this piece I use a 5-6-7 (7 being the bass) for the opening G chord. In the 1-5-1 tuning, any chord can be inverted. Therefore a 5-6-7 chord could be played 7-6-5 (5 being the bass). The 5-5-7 Bm chord can be played 7-5-5 — and so on. It all depends on the voicing you wish to achieve. Experiment and find out what sounds best on your instrument.

A Week in January: By the multi-talented instrumentalist Seamus Egan, from the album of the same name on Shanachie Records #65005. If the hammers and pulls are too many and too fast, just pick out the melody at first till you become comfortable with the tune. Seamus' album is beautiful and inspiring and I highly recommend it.

American Landscape: I composed this piece with the Amish country of Eastern Pennsylvania in mind: the beautiful farms, the rolling hills and the simple way of life. I use my thumb a lot, so I start the tune with my middle finger over the second fret and my thumb over the fourth. A rip (R) is done by dragging one's (fretting) finger across all the strings, bass to treble.

Andante from the *Quartet in A Major* (Wolfgang Amadeus Mozart, 1756-1791): Why am I arranging this piece in A major in D? As mentioned above, D-A-D is the tuning of choice these days. To play this in A one would have to tune A-E-A which would mean tuning your strings so high they would break or so low they would sound terrible. I've recently purchased a very small "box" dulcimer and put very thin strings on it (.008 - .011 - .018W) so I could play in this key. I like to use a flatpick and articulate near the bridge to get the most "bite".

Appaloosa (Hellman/Weed): Arranged for the happy flatpicker. Play this one in slow motion at first. Try to master a small phrase at a time. I must admit I still have trouble with this one but it's worth the work.

Arkansas Traveler: From an old medicine show skit, this classic utilizes a combination of strums and single note picking. Please feel free to arrange this in your own style.

Arran Boat Song: A good example of playing in the Dorian mode while in the 1-5-1 tuning. Though you are tuned D-A-D you are playing this Scottish melody in the Dorian of E (Em). I start this tune out with my ring, middle and index fingers over the first, second and bass strings respectively. One could put a capo over the first fret and play the numbers on the first string. Another method would be to tune: C-A-D (D being the bass) and play the numbers you see on the first string. The key, however would change to Dm.

Beauty in Tears (Turlough O'Carolan, 1670-1738): One of over 2,000 pieces arranged for the harp by the legendary Irish bard. Shortly after he was blinded by smallpox at the age of eighteen, Turlough was given instruction on the harp by a member of the MacDermott Roe family. O'Carolan lived during one the worst periods of Irish history. In the era of Cromwell, Catholics in Ireland were denied almost all civil rights including free speech, the right to choose a profession, even the right to inherit your own family's land. This and many other unbearable laws drove over 150,000 of the best Irish youth to flee the country between 1690-1730, an exodus known as the Flight of the Wild Geese. This was the environment in which O'Carolan lived and wrote harp music which now, almost 300 years later, is played and enjoyed as it was the day it was written. It should be noted that there were other harpers at this time including David Murphey, Cornelius Lyons and Myles O'Reilly, to name a few. Much of their work can be found in *The Bunting Collection*. For further reading and more O'Carolan compositions, try to find *The Life and Times of the Irish Harper* by Donal O'Sullivan, published in 1958.

Bagatelle: I wrote this *Bagatelle* as a fun piece and promptly used it as the theme for the children's video fairy tale *Princess Furball*. As in many of the compositions, I employ a flatpick to articulate the notes. I also like to use my thumb, especially pulling from 5-3-3 to 3 (see bar #3).

Betty Likens: In this tuning, the bass is taken way down to A. If you're in D-A-D, just lower the bass string till it's an octave below the middle string. This is a great tuning for all those modal tunes in the key of A. Try to angle your pick so as not to "drone" out the melody. Start with your ring, middle and index fingers over the seventh, eighth and ninth fret of the melody string.

Bianco Fiori: Notice in bar #3, I play the full chords. Perhaps you should try a variation: just play the melody string for a different tone on your second time through this Renaissance dance tune.

Blind Mary: O'Carolan composed this sad and pretty air for his friend Mary Dhall. The 6+-4-3 chord adds a bit more poignancy to the piece.

Boatin' Up Sandy: Same type of tune as *Betty Likens.* Flatpicker extraordinaire Norman Blake plays this tune as *Weave and Way.*

Bonaparte Crossing the Rhine and **Bonaparte's Retreat:** These two go very well together as a medley. The *Rhine* is a good example of playing in the Ionian mode while tuned 1-5-1. Since you have a C# on the second fret middle string you can play a tune in the Ionian mode without going higher than the fifth fret.

Canarios: This piece by Gaspar Sanz (1640-1710) is probably one of the most difficult in the book. I like to play it on my small dulcimer in the key of G. There are many versions of this composition. I learned this one from the talented guitarist William Coulter.

The Chanter's Song: As in *Arran Boat Song,* this arrangement is for the Dorian of E while tuned to D-A-D. The chanter refers to the part of the pipes where the melody is played. I played this version on *The Fairie Round* by Shelley Phillips (Gourd Music #105).

Cluck Old Hen: Once again in a mountain minor of D-A-A (A being the bass). I must comment here that I find this song's lyrics rather confusing. First, the hen is laying eggs generously for the railroad men — then the narrator complains of her not laying since late last fall or even spring. Very mystifying indeed.

The Cuckoo: The cuckoo bird is a symbol of infidelity. This version is different than its well-known American cousin. I learned this arrangement from the playing of the group Pentangle.

Cumha Eoghain Rua Ui Neill: O'Carolan's lament for Owen Roe O'Neill, who was a nephew of the great Earl of Tyrone and led the Irish to a victory over General Monroe's Anglo-Scottish army at Benburb in 1646. His death three years later marked the end of the Irish hope of defeating Cromwell. I learned this version from the playing of the group Clannad.

The Dark Forest: Also known as *The Forest of Garth,* here is another D-A-A (A being the bass) arrangement. I learned it many years ago from the playing of the great British Columbia band The Pied Pumpkin.

Douce Dame: Medieval master Guillaume de Machaut composed this haunting melody in the Dorian mode for his young mistress.

Durango: I wrote this piece for 4 equi-distant strings tuned D-D-G-D. It is my hope that you, too, will appreciate this tuning. It's wonderful to compose in and as you can see, there are many chord possibilities that do not exist in 3 string tunings. All the fret numbers that do not have notes above them in the musical staff are eighth notes (as in bars #3, 12, 25 and 26). Try just playing the back up chords at first. The chords are written out to show you finger position for each bar. In other words, for bars 1 and 3, you would hold down the 3-0-2-3 chord and for bars 5 and 6, you'd hold down the 1-0-3-3 chord.

El Tutu: Tuned D-G-D, a sort of "new" Ionian Mode of G, whose advantage is that one can play the same melody on the bass string as on the treble string. Each of the three parts has a different rhythm. Learned from the playing of the group Calliope from the album *Calliope Festival,* Nonesuch Records #79069.

Fiddlin' Bagpipes: I learned this old time East Tennessee mountain tune from Jean Schilling. A fun way to play it would be to tune all the strings of the dulcimer to the same note (A-A-A or B-B-B). As in *Betty Likens,* start with your ring, middle and index fingers over the 7th, 8th and 9th fret of the melody string. A harmonic is where you place your finger over the said fret, strum across and lift at the same time to produce a "chime" like tone.

Fisher's Hornpipe: I found this in a book titled *Social Music in Colonial Boston* by Barbara Lambert. This version came to America of a composition by James A. Fishar, who was the musical director at Covent Garden in London in the 1770's. It's recorded on *The World Turned Upside Down* by Barry Phillips (GM #110).

Foggy Dew: Here's another example of playing in G while tuned D-A-D. I do like to lead with my thumb. If you adhere to Lorraine Lee school of dulcimer playing, and don't like to use your thumb, please feel free to alter the arrangement to suit your own type of fingering.

Gaelic Air: This beautiful air is from the playing of Alasdair Fraser and Paul Machlis on their record, *The Road North,* Sona Gaia #155. Please note that to play a low C natural I needed to utilize the 6th fret of the bass string. I have seen a number of folks who have put a 1.5 fret on their dulcimers which would help with a tune like this.

The Girl I Left Behind Me: Needless to say one does not have to do all the hammers and pulls, but it does make the arrangement more dynamic.

God Rest Ye Merry, Gentleman: In this arrangement we are playing in Bm while tuned to D-A-D, illustrating that one can play in the Aeolian of B while in a D tuning. Please notice our merry gentlemen are dancing in jig time (6/8), which is a great tempo for this melody.

Hewlett: This beautiful baroque air by O'Carolan is a bit tricky, but there are many recorded versions available to inspire you. I like playing this with a flatpick to articulate the melody.

I Am a Little Scholar: Be sure to tune Bb-F-C (C being the bass) to play this haunting gospel tune. Learned at the Carter Family Festival in Hiltons, Virginia many years ago.

I've Been All Around This World: This great banjo song apparently pertains to Judge Isaac Parker, who in the latter part of the 19th century sent many a man to his greater reward at Ft. Smith, Arkansas.

Kingdom Coming: Though you may not recognize the title, you've heard this melody in countless movies about the Civil War and that time period. Written by H.C. Work in around 1862, I learned this from the album *Gala* by Carole Koenig.

La Mort de Coucy: I wrote this lament for Enguerrand de Coucy VII, hero of the book *A Distant Mirror* by Barbara Tuchman, which chronicles the calamitous 14th century — an era of endless warfare, political and religious scandals and diseases that could not be cured — imagine living in such a time. Arranged for fingerpicking, please play this one slowly.

The Lakes of Pontchartrain: I learned this from the singing of Paul Brady. Although the arrangement includes the melody, I prefer to just play the back-up chords and sing this long sad Irish ballad about love lost in Louisiana.

Lauda: The *Lauda* is a song of devotion which first flowered in Italy, probably around the time of St. Francis (1182-1226). The *Laudas* from the 14th century are associated with the flagellants of Northern Italy who sang *laude spirituali* in their processions. For this arrangement, I would use a simple "pinch-pick" pattern. Pinch with your thumb and middle finger and pick the middle string with your index finger. The pick on the middle string is always an eighth note which would make the number played before it an eighth note as well — meaning that all the numbers you play in bar #1 are eighth notes. This first 0 on the middle string is not notated on the musical staff because it is really not part of the melody.

Lauda Di Maria Maddalenna: This slow song of praise is much in the style of *La Mort de Coucy*. As you can see, I like to arrange in Bm while tuned to D-A-D. Both *Laudas* were learned from the merry harper Kim Robertson.

Little St. Anne: Joe Weed and I wrote this advanced piece for a handicapped girl I used to take care of during my year as an aide in special education. Try learning this one part at a time.

Loch Lavan Castle: Here's another minor key arrangement while tuned to D-A-D which I learned from the playing of Teddy McKnight, a lover of those spooky celtoid tunes.

Lord Franklin: This song is the sad tale of Admiral Sir John Franklin, who disappeared in the Arctic in 1859 trying to find the Northwest Passage. It's arranged for four equidistant strings — try doing a simple fingerpicking pattern through the back-up chords which for this ballad are written on the dulcimer tab.

Minuet (J.S. Bach, 1685-1750): First Mozart, now Bach... how do you arrange a minuet composed in G in the key of D? If you want to play it in the correct key for this 1-5-1 tuning you will have to tune G-D-G. Needless to say this will be too high or too low for a dulcimer that is usually tuned to D-A-D. I have a mini dulcimer as explained above for just such an occasion.

Morrison's Jig: Notice that you can play this Dorian fiddle piece while tuned 1-5-1 without ever going past the fourth fret.

Neal's Maggot: A maggot is a dance tune and, well, I just had to learn this one. Special thanks to Cece Webster for sending me the music.

Ninety-Pound Catfish: I wrote this rip-roaring dulcimer tune while on tour in Tennessee, and it's based on a true story. I tried to sell it to television for a mini-series but they just refused to pay me scale. Note the modulation to the key of G.

Now My Dear Companions: This is a Shaker hymn transcribed by Augustus P. Bless around the time of the Civil War. It is recorded on the album *Simple Gifts* (Gourd Music #106).

Pavane for a Sleeping Beauty *(Pavane de la belle au bois dormant):* This is a movement from the *Mother Goose Suite (Ma mère l'oye)* written in 1908 by Maurice Ravel (1875-1937). If some of the chords — like 9-9-11 — are too awkward, try just playing the melody note.

Picnic on the St. Croix: This is another tune I wrote for four equidistant strings tuned D-D-G-D. As in *Durango,* the chords are written out to show you finger position for each bar.

Planxty Eleanor Plunkett: O'Carolan wrote a number of pieces for the Plunkett family. The popular story is that Eleanor was the only survivor of the Plunkett family's insane attempt to boil themselves to death in their castle. Played in G while tuned D-A-D.

Planxty George Brabazon: Brabazon was probably a patron of O'Carolan. Interestingly, O'Carolan's biographer Sullivan contends in *The Life and Times of the Irish Harper* that the bard did not use the term *Planxty* as copiously as it has been ascribed to him. *Planxty* can mean "in honor of" or "in praise of" a certain patron, but as Sullivan states "...the planxty is a harp tune of sportive and animated character, not intended for, or often adaptable to, words; and with the exception of three or four tunes to which possibly the term has been incorrectly applied it moves in triplets, with a six-eight measure..."

Robertson's Unreel: I wrote this jig for my harper friend and world traveler Kim Robertson.

Rondeau (Jean Mouret 1682-1738): Mouret, court composer for Louis XIV, achieved immortality with this work when it was adopted as the theme for television's Masterpiece Theatre. This version contains all four parts.

Sailor's Alphabet: I learned this great singalong song over twenty years ago from the singing of David Axler. It's by Fairport Convention, and is recorded on their *"Babbacombe" Lee* album.

Sheebeg and Sheemore: This classic O'Carolan composition tells of the love of the big hill and the little hill which have grown out of the head and heart of the slain knight Finn McCool. The little fairie folk who live on the hills, however, are at war.

Spagnoletta: Praetorius (1569-1621) may have brought this popular dance tune of the day from Italy to Germany while he was kapellmeister to the Duke of Brunswick. If you'd like to play this just on one string, re-tune to C-A-D and just play the numbers on the first string. Of course you will now be in the key of Dm instead of Em.

Road to Lisdoonvarna: This is one of the first Irish tunes I learned. Once again, you will be playing in the Dorian of E while tuned to D-A-D.

Young William Plunkett: O'Carolan named this work for another member of the mad Plunkett family. It is somewhat difficult, so please play it through slowly at first.

UNDERSTANDING THE TABLATURE

Tablature is much easier than reading music because what you see is a just a picture of the dulcimer. There is one line for each string, and the line closest to you is the string closest to you. The number tells you which fret to play. "0" means to play the string open. If there are 2 or more numbers right on top of each other, as at the beginning of this song, it means to play all of the notes at the same time. A curved line between the numbers signifies an ornamentation.

There are four ways to ornament, and they play an important part in giving the dulcimer its characteristic sound. "H" means to hammer on; "P" means to pull off; "SL" means to slide; "R" means to rip across all the strings.

The conventional music above the tablature is simply the melody — in standard musical notation. It also shows the rhythm. Sometimes there will be tablature notes with no conventional notes above them. These are fingerpicking notes which fall between the melody notes. **They are always eighth notes.** To make life even easier, the backup chords above the music have three numbers next to them. They tell you which frets to use to play the chords.

AMERICAN LANDSCAPE

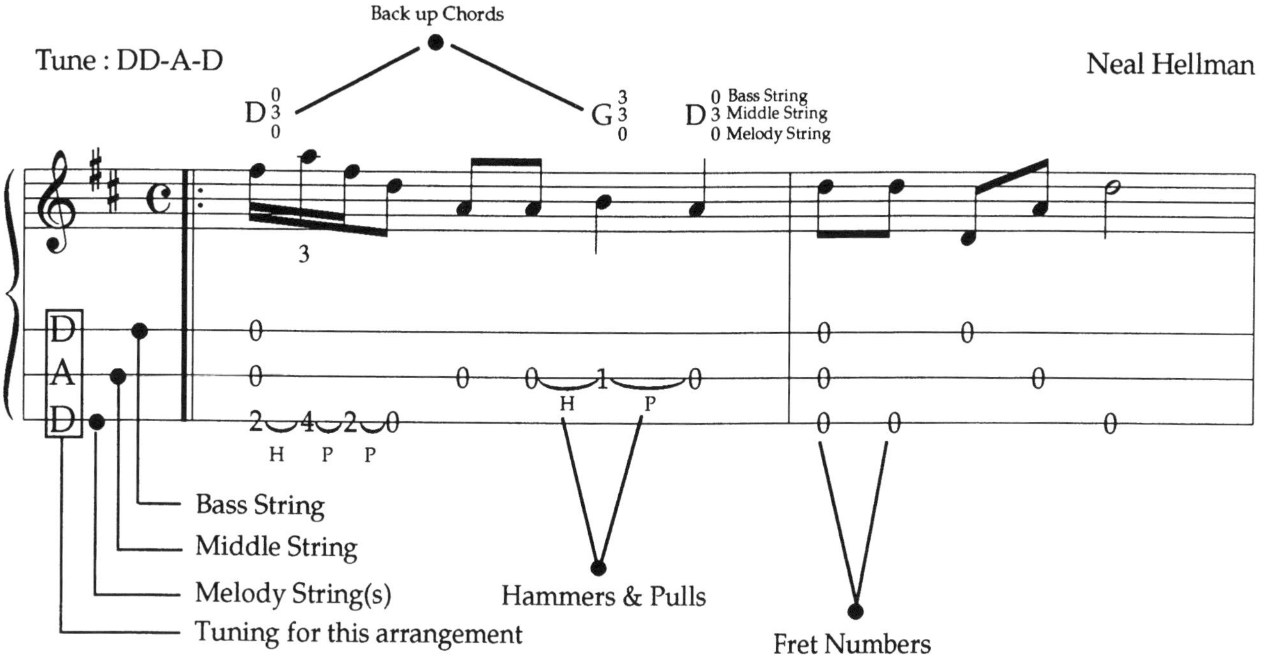

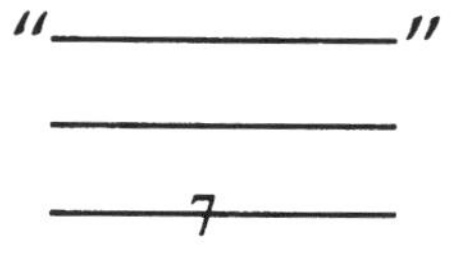

means play the 7th fret of the melody string

Just play what you see!

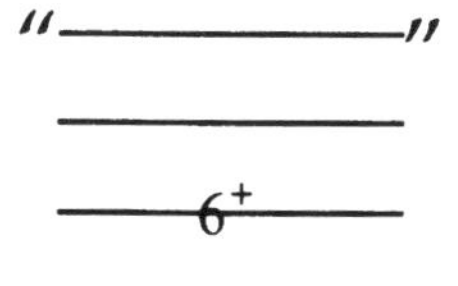

means play the extra fret between the 6th & 7th fret of the melody string

Articulations: "H" = Hammer ON
"P" = Pull OFF
"SL" = Slide
"R" = Rip

A SONG FOR LORI

Tune : DD-A-D

Hellman-Weed

Em Am G Dsus D
Am G D Am Bm
D D G
Bm Am D G

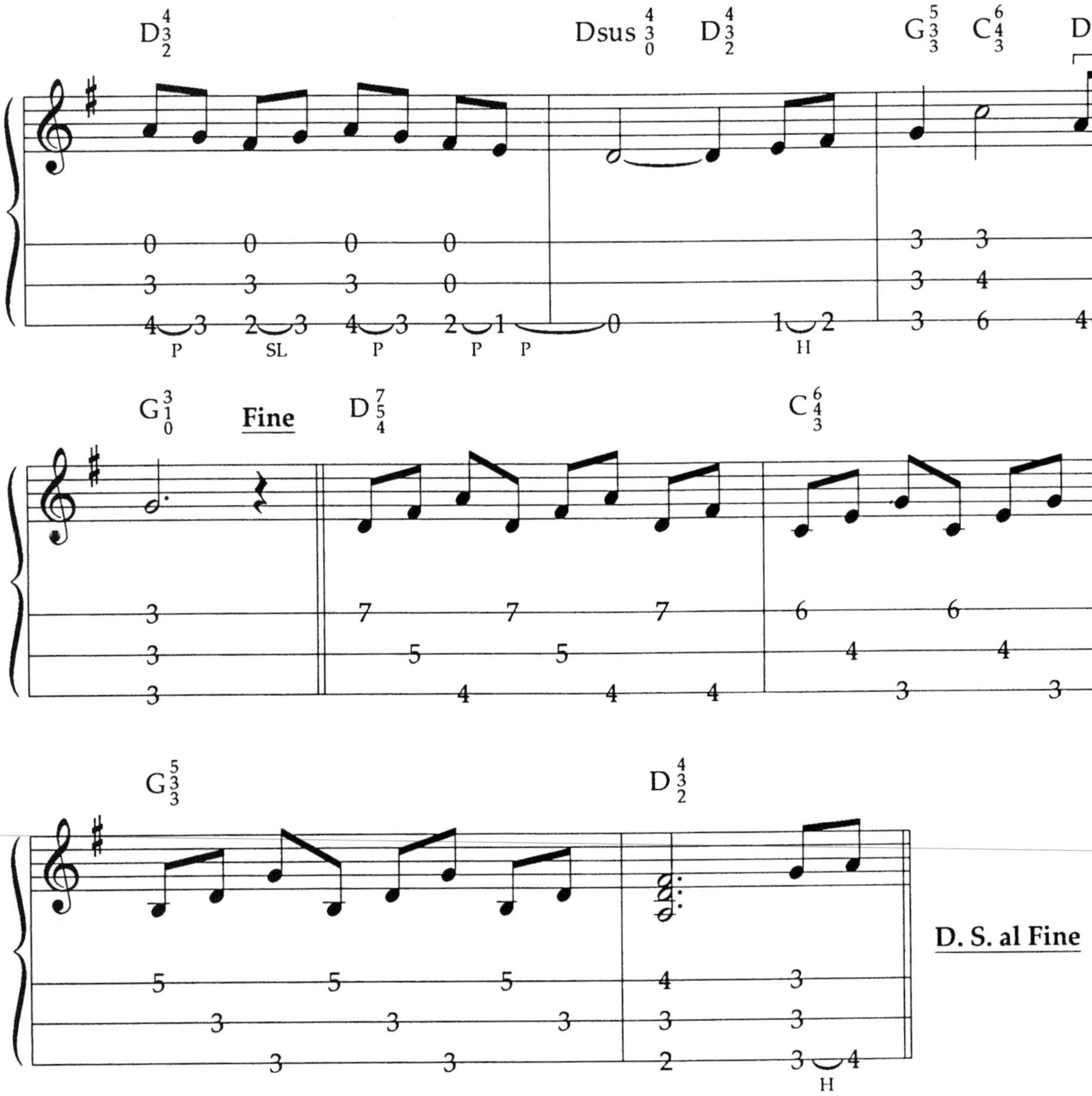
D
Dsus
D
G
C
D
G
Fine
D
C
G
D
D. S. al Fine

A WEEK IN JANUARY

Tune : DD-A-D

Seamus Egan

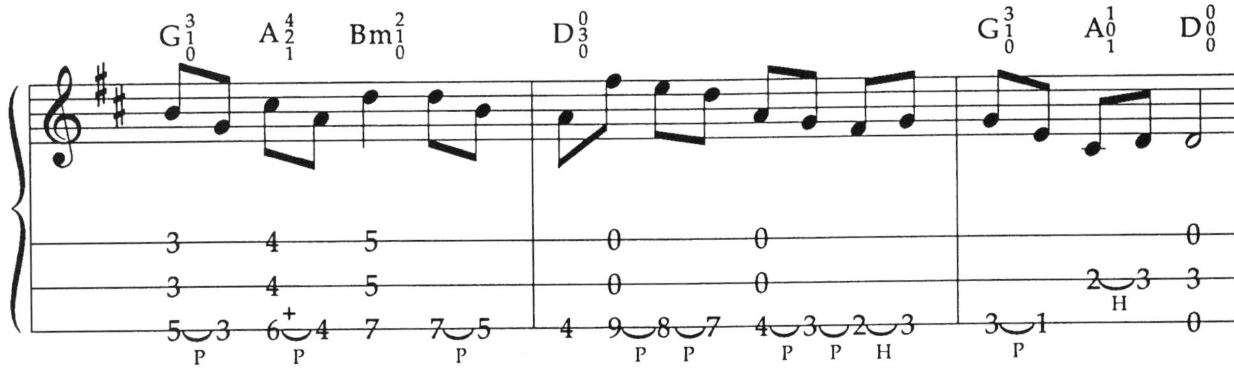

G
A
Bm
D
G
A
D
P
P
P
P
P
P
P
H
P
H

AMERICAN LANDSCAPE

Tune : DD-A-D

Neal Hellman

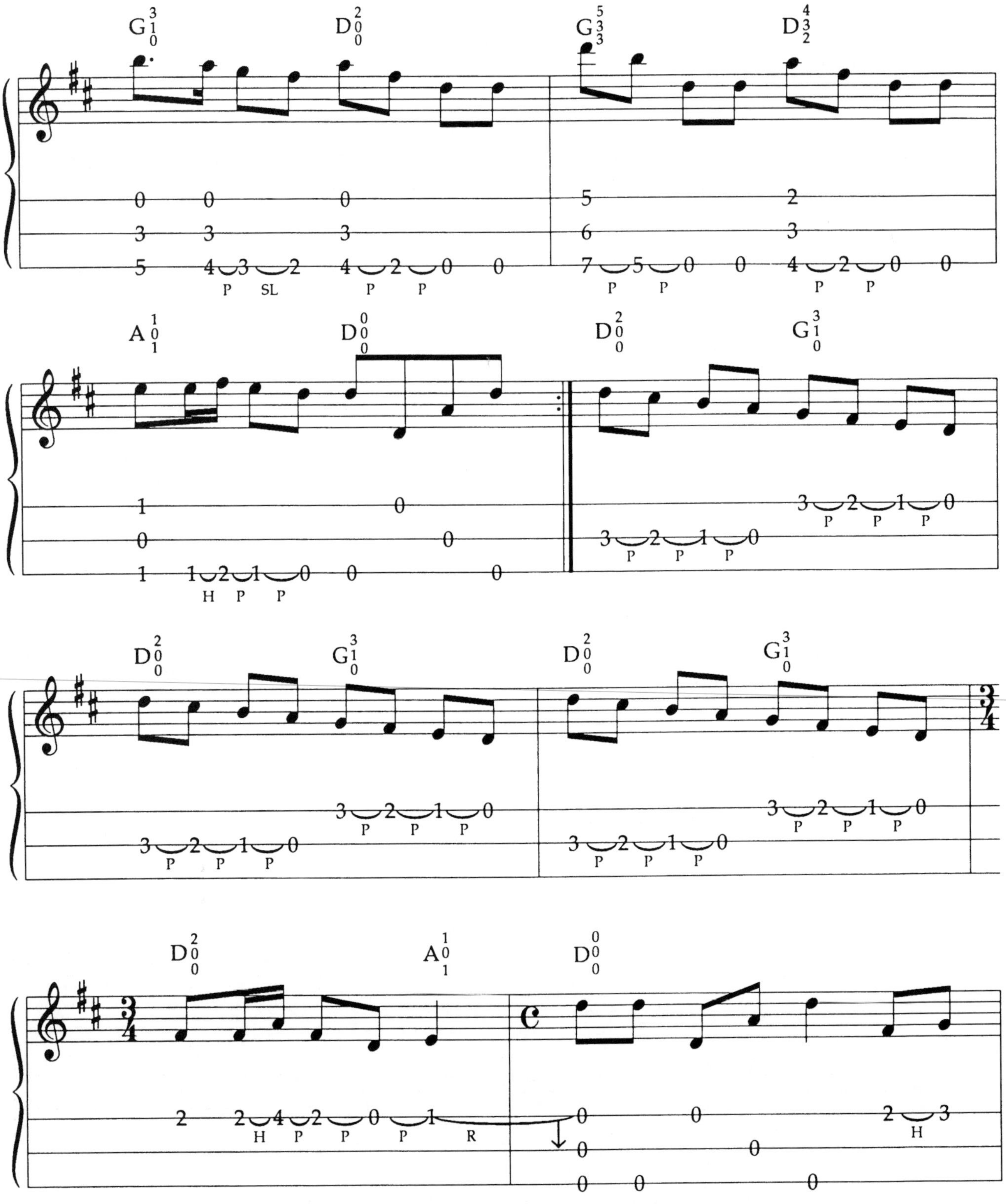
G D G D
A D D G
D G D G
D A D

D A
D A D A
D
D G D G
D A D D G D G D A D
H P R

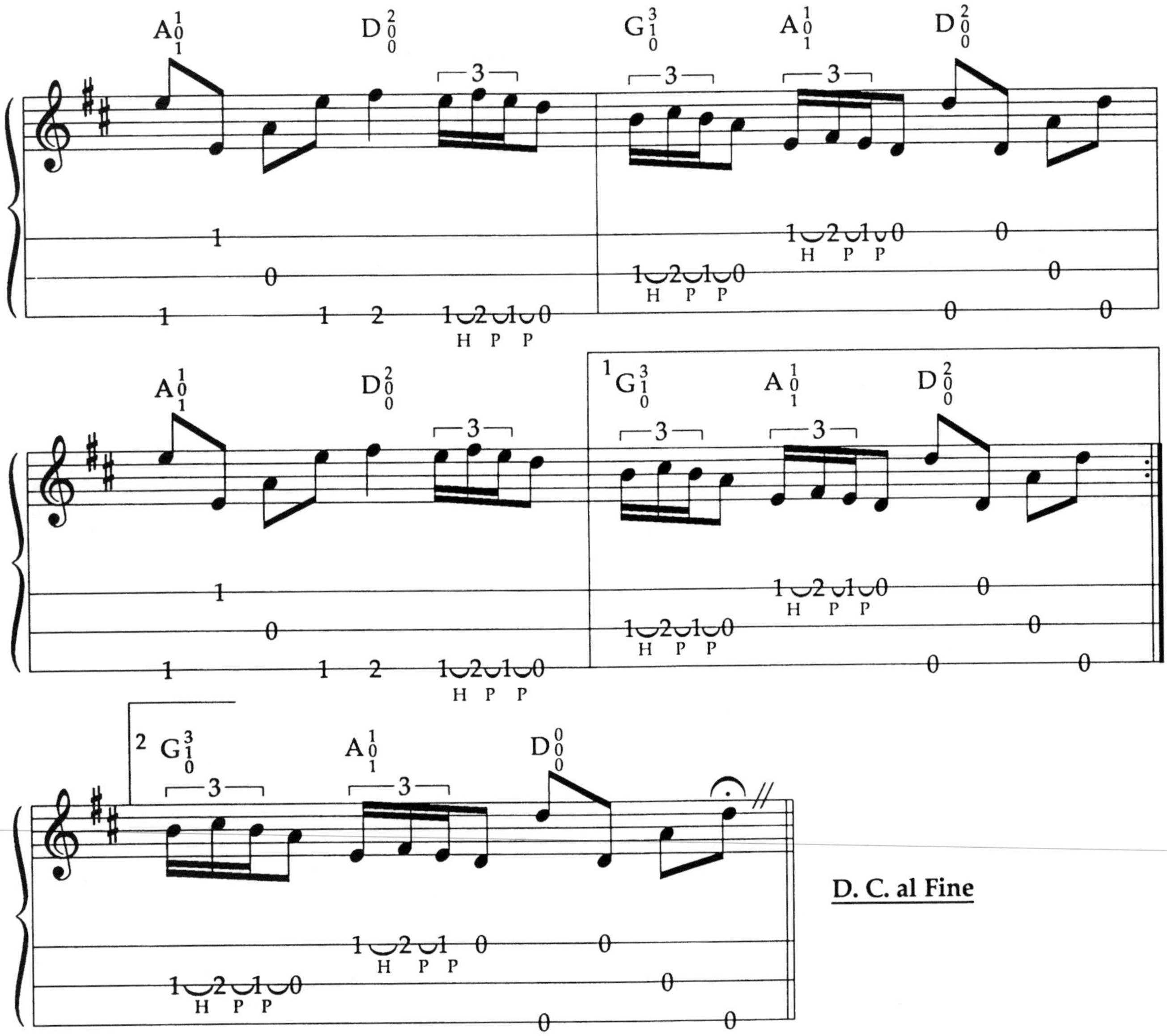
A
D
G
A
D
A
D
G
A
D
G
A
D
H P P
D. C. al Fine

ANDANTE FROM QUARTET IN A MAJOR

(K298)

Tune : DD-A-D

Wolfgang Amadeus Mozart
(1756-1791)

APPALOOSA

Tune : DD-A-D

Hellman-Weed

A
D
Bm
G
D
1 A
D
2 A
D
D
A
D
D

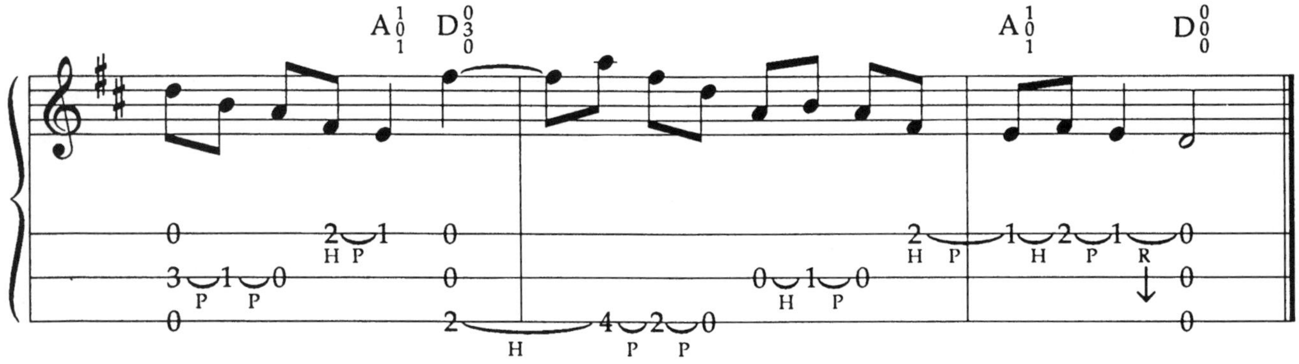
A D A D

ARKANSAS TRAVELER

Tune : DD-A-D

Traditional

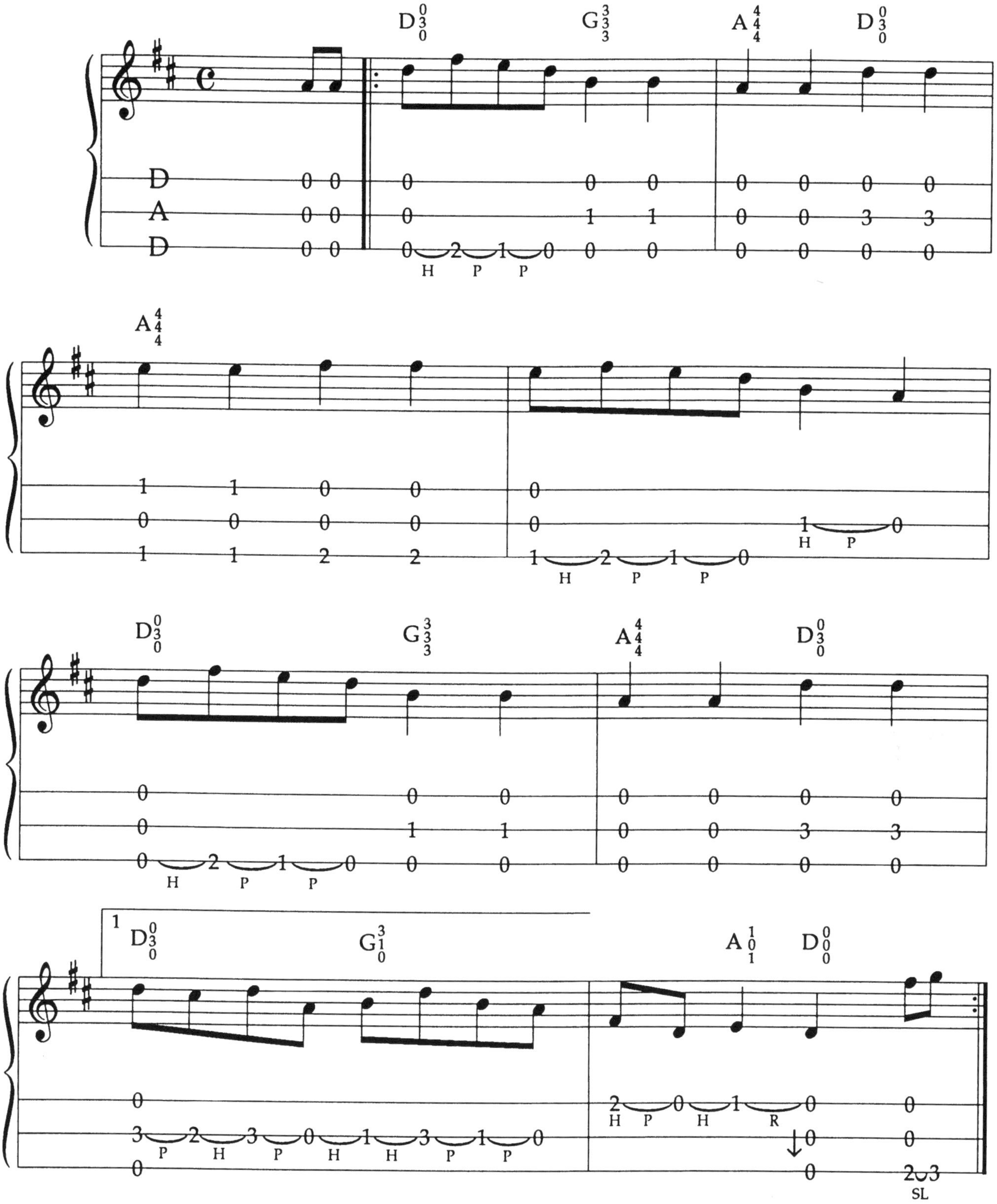

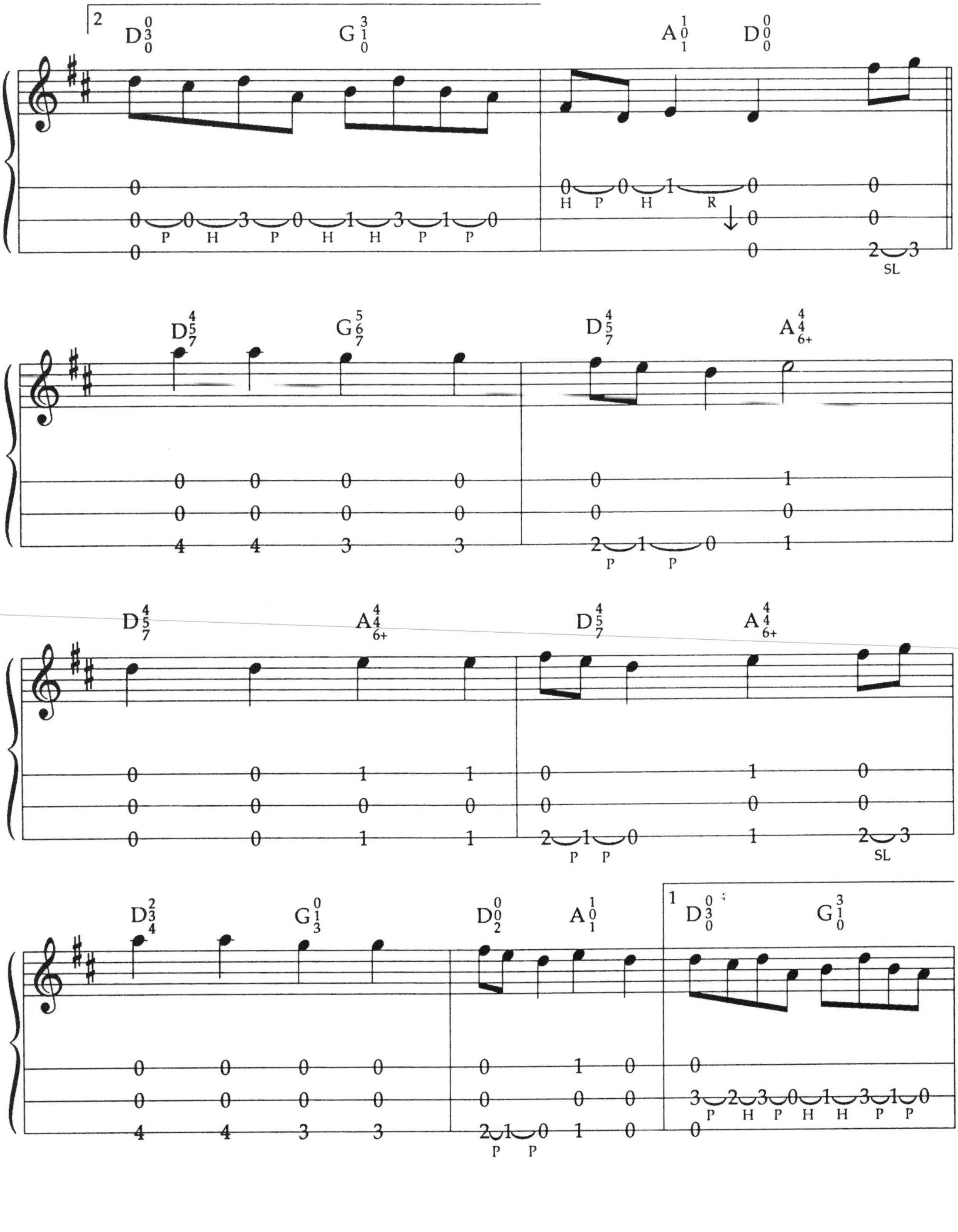

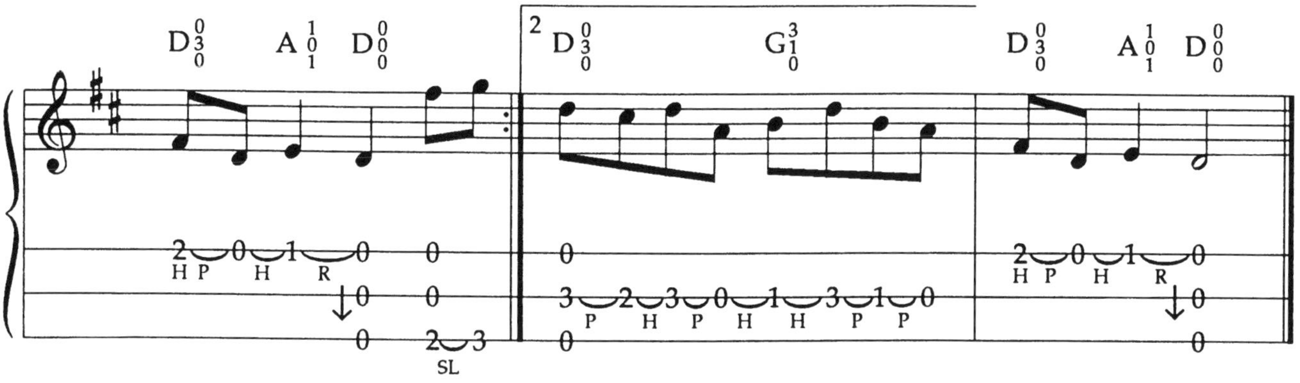

Though it is not done very often, there is an old medicine show skit that goes along with the tune. The traveler who is trying to find his way to Arkansas becomes the straight man for the joking farmer. Play the "A" part, perform the joke, then the "B" part. That's just one way to do it; work it out as you like.

Traveler (T): Which one of these roads do I take to Arkansas?
Farmer (F): No need to, they already have one there.

T: Is that creek fordable?
F: My neighbor's ducks forded it this morning.

T: I mean, how deep is it?
F: Water all the way to the bottom.

T: Have you lived here all your life?
F: Not yet.

T: How did your potatoes turn out this year?
F: The devil, they didn't turn out. Me and my wife had to dig 'em out.

T: Say, farmer, your roof needs mending. Why don't you mend your roof?
F: Can't mend it while it's raining, and when it's not raining, it don't leak.

T: Say, your wife's dress is mighty short.
F: It'll be long enough before she gets a new one.

T: That's a mighty big horse over there, have any trouble getting down off a' him?
F: Round here, friend, we only get down off a duck.

ARRAN BOAT SONG

Tune : DD-A-D

Traditional Scottish

*The phrase: 5 6+ 7 can be played 1 2 3 on the middle string if you don't have the extra fret.

BAGATELLE

Tune : DD-A-D

Neal Hellman

BEAUTY IN TEARS

Tune : DD-A-D

Turlough O'Carolan
(1670-1738)

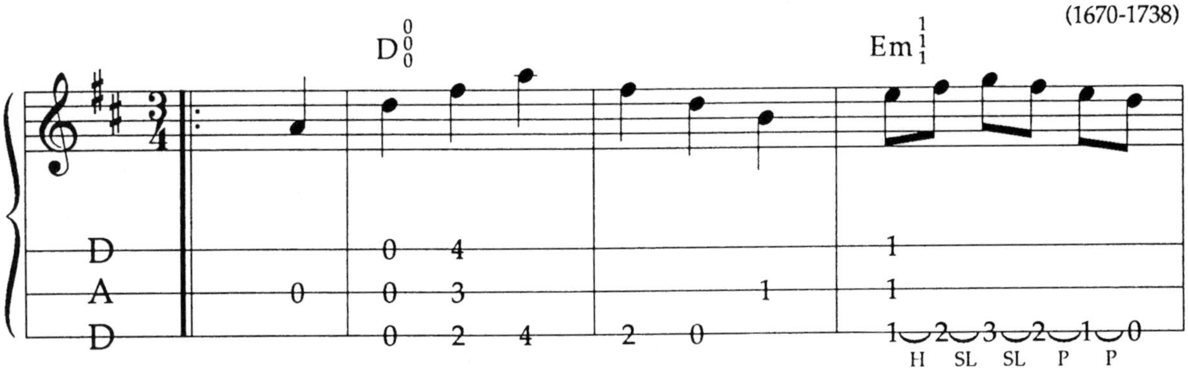

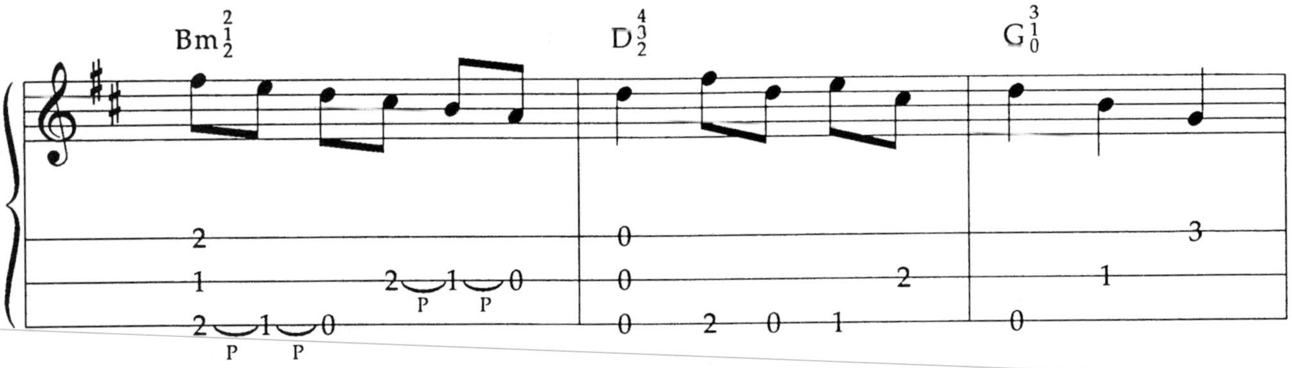

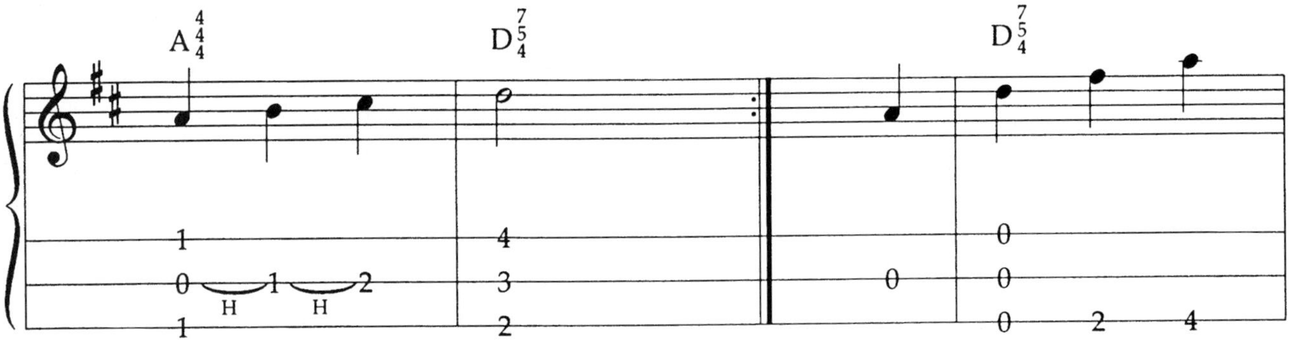

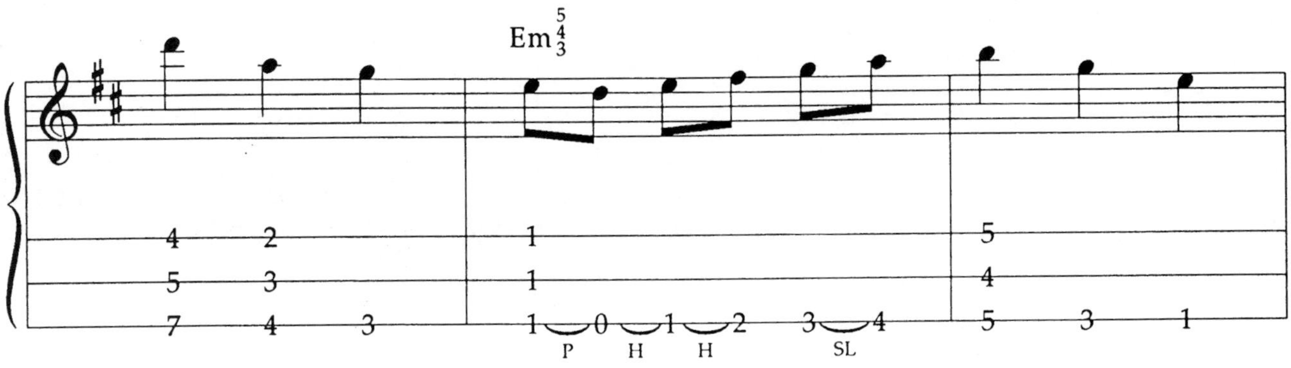

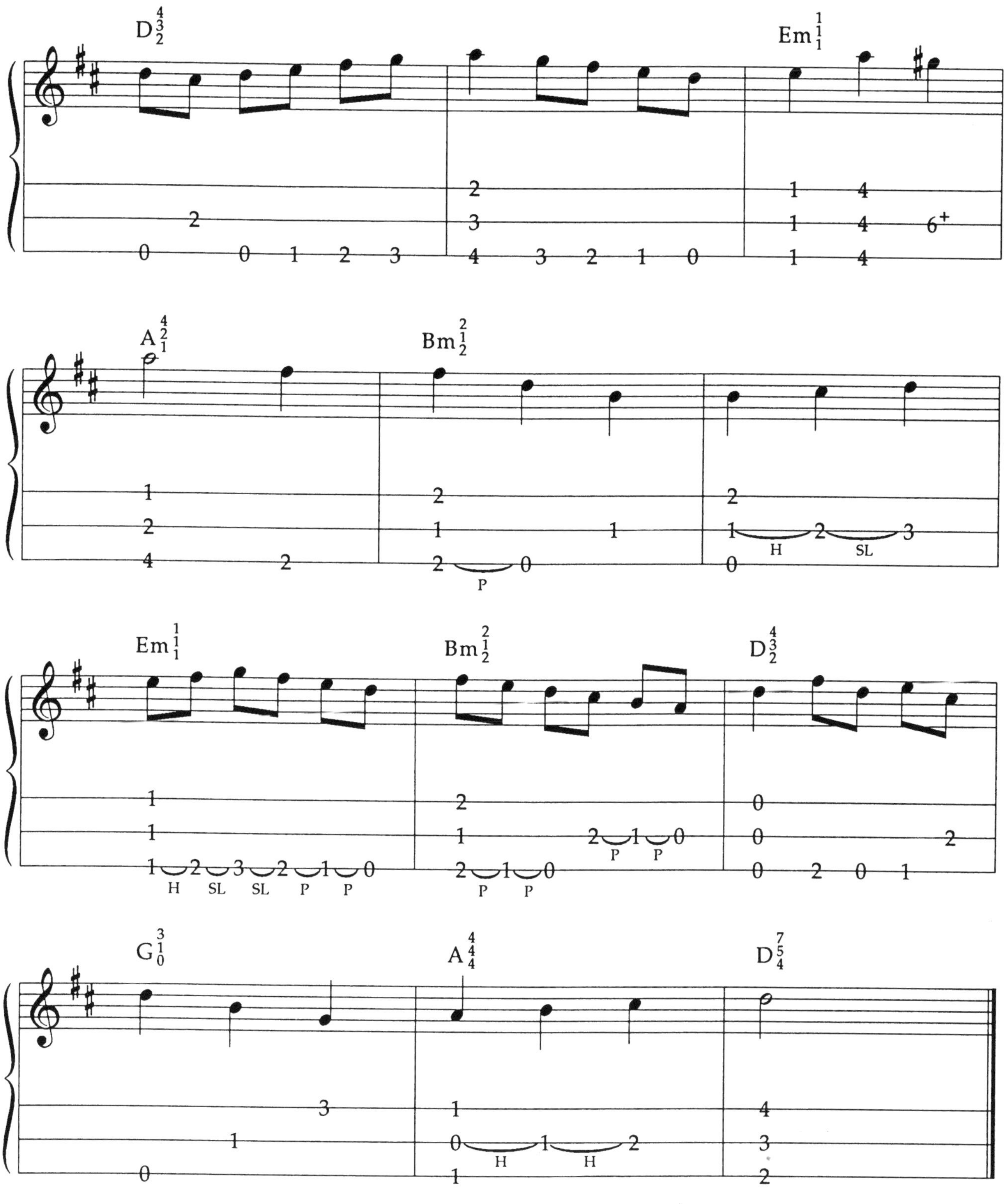
D
Em
A
Bm
Em
Bm
D
G
A
D

BETTY LIKENS

Tune : DD-A-A

Traditional

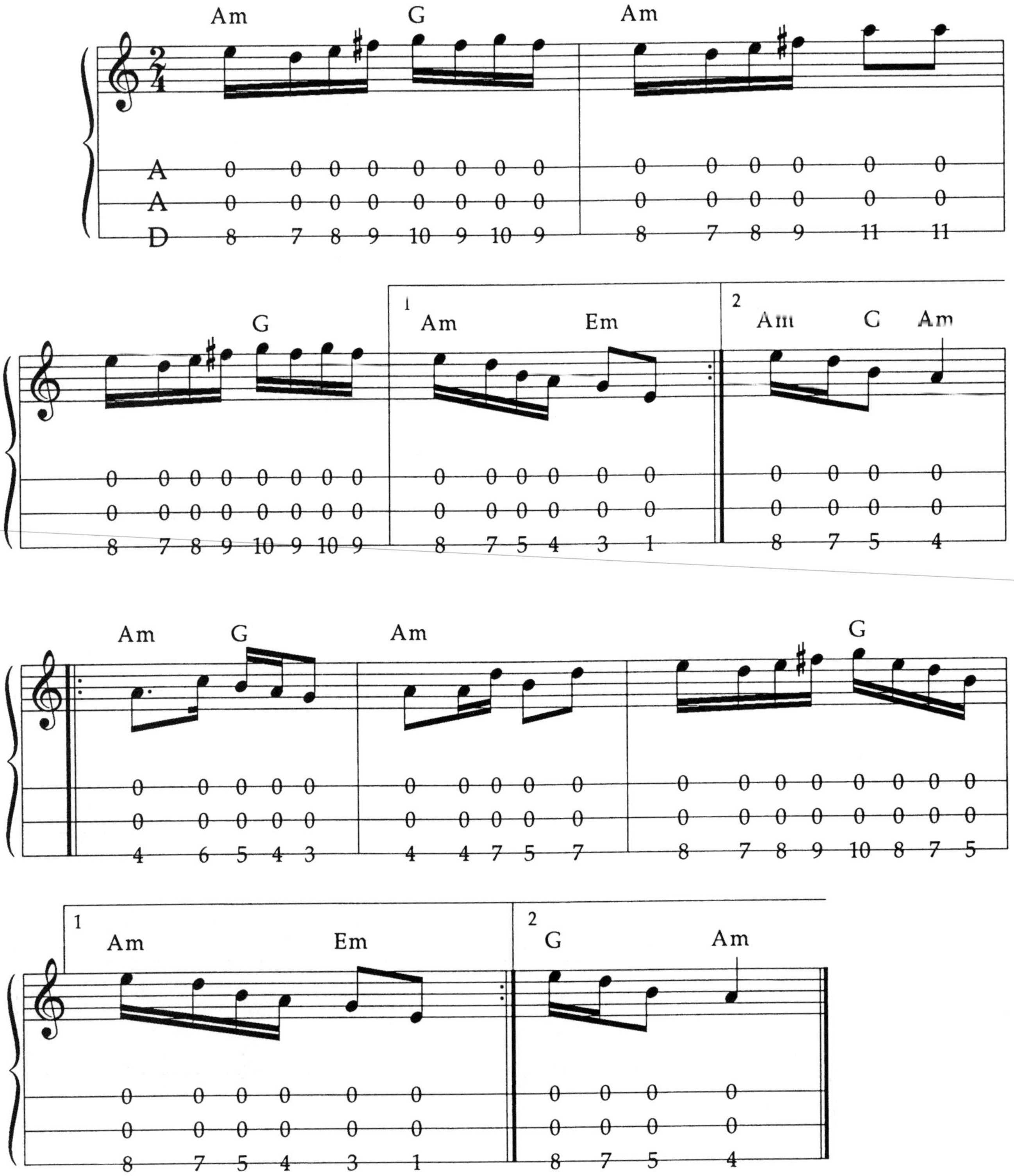

BIANCO FIORI

Tune : DD-A-D

Trad. Italian

If playing the bass string 6th fret is too awkward use the 2nd fret middle string.

BLIND MARY

Tune : DD-A-D

Turlough O'Carolan
(1670-1738)

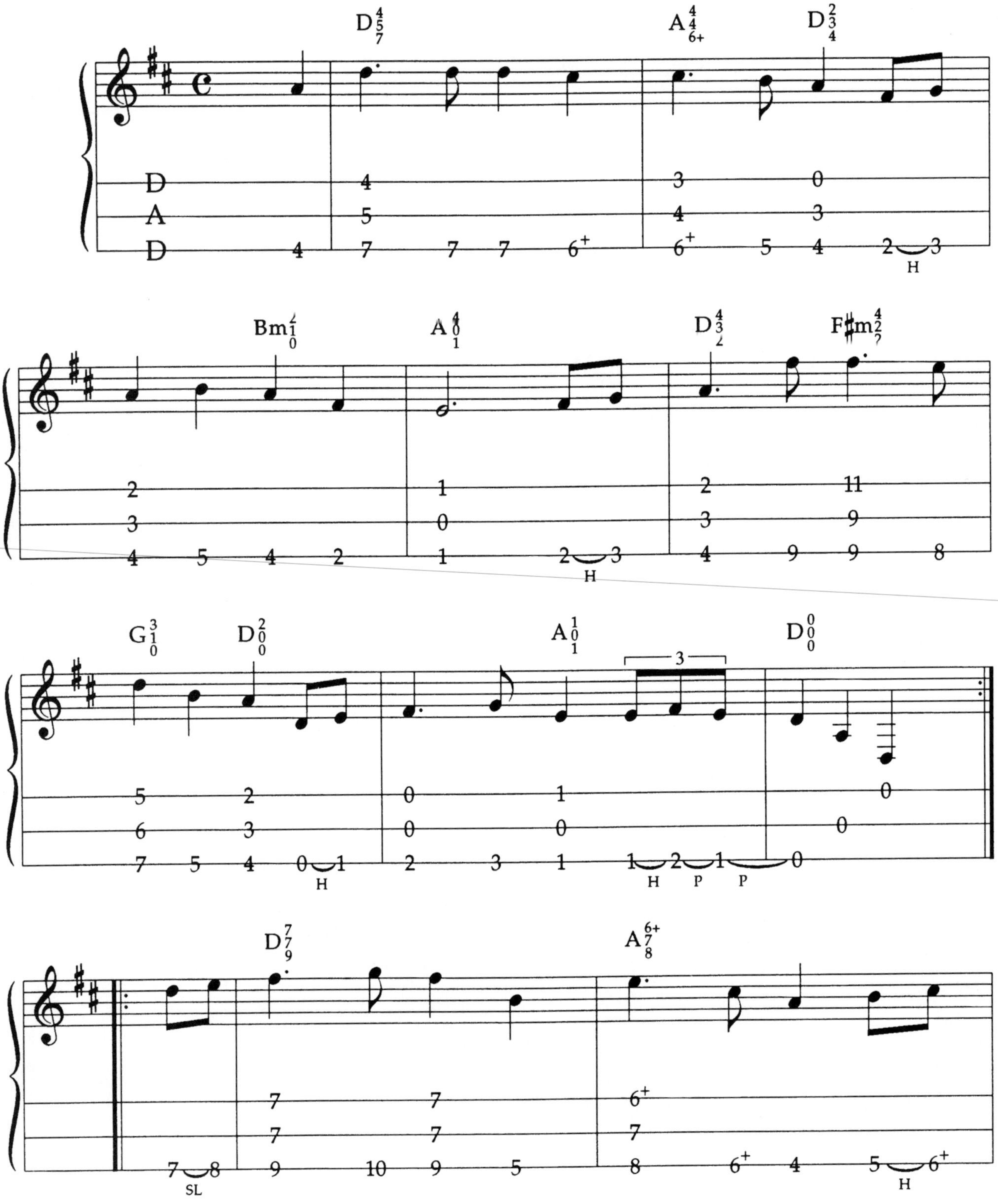

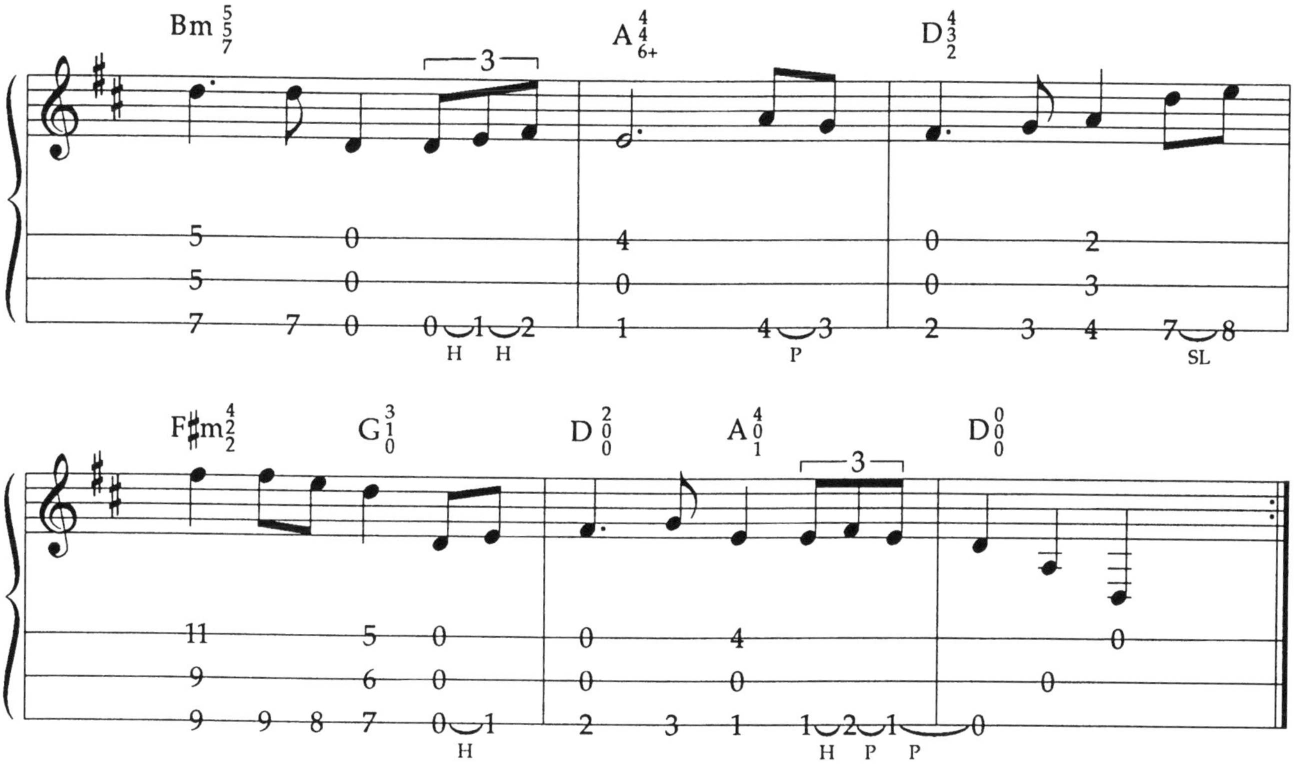
Bm
A
D
F♯m
G
D
A
D
H
P
SL

BOATIN' UP SANDY

(WEAVE AND WAY)

Tune : DD-A-A

Traditional Fiddle Tune

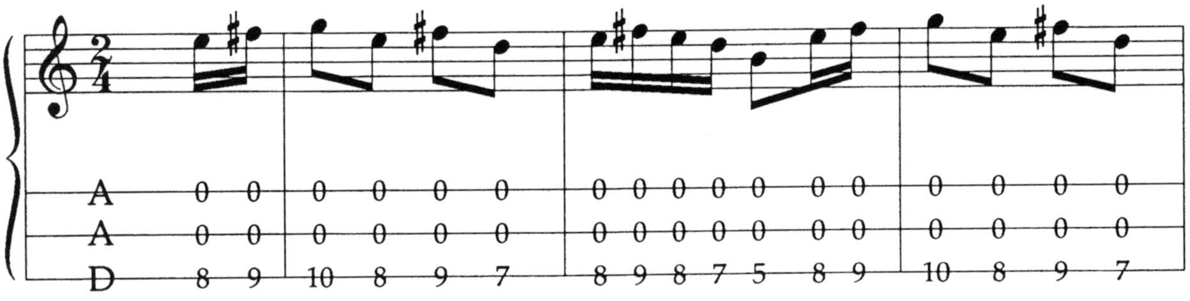

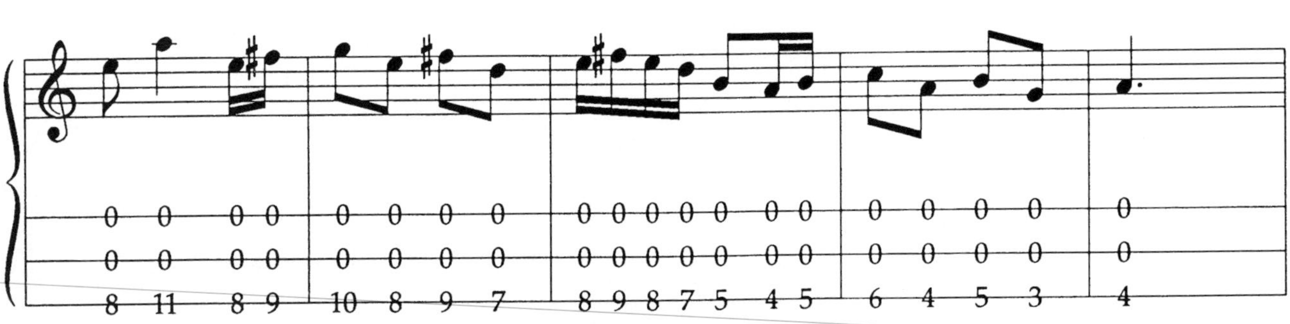

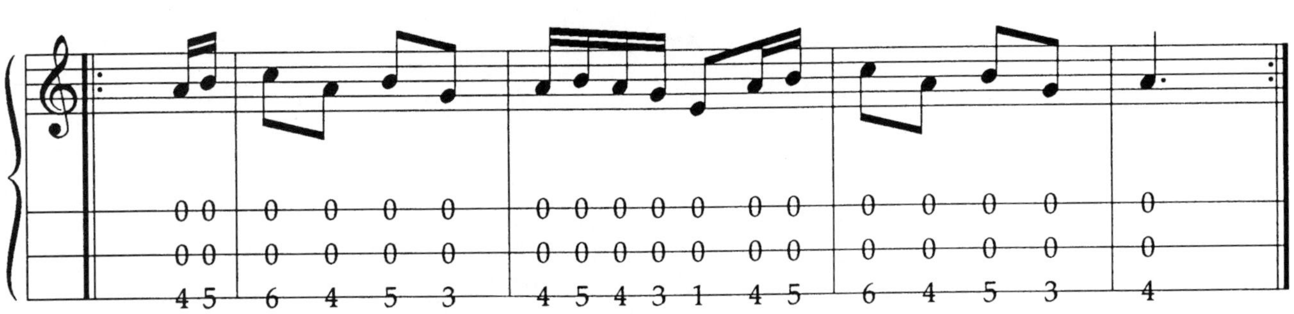

Start out with your ring finger on the 8th fret, middle finger on the 9th and index finger on the 10th fret, as if you were playing three keys on the piano.

BONAPARTE CROSSING THE RHINE

Tune : DD-A-D

Traditional

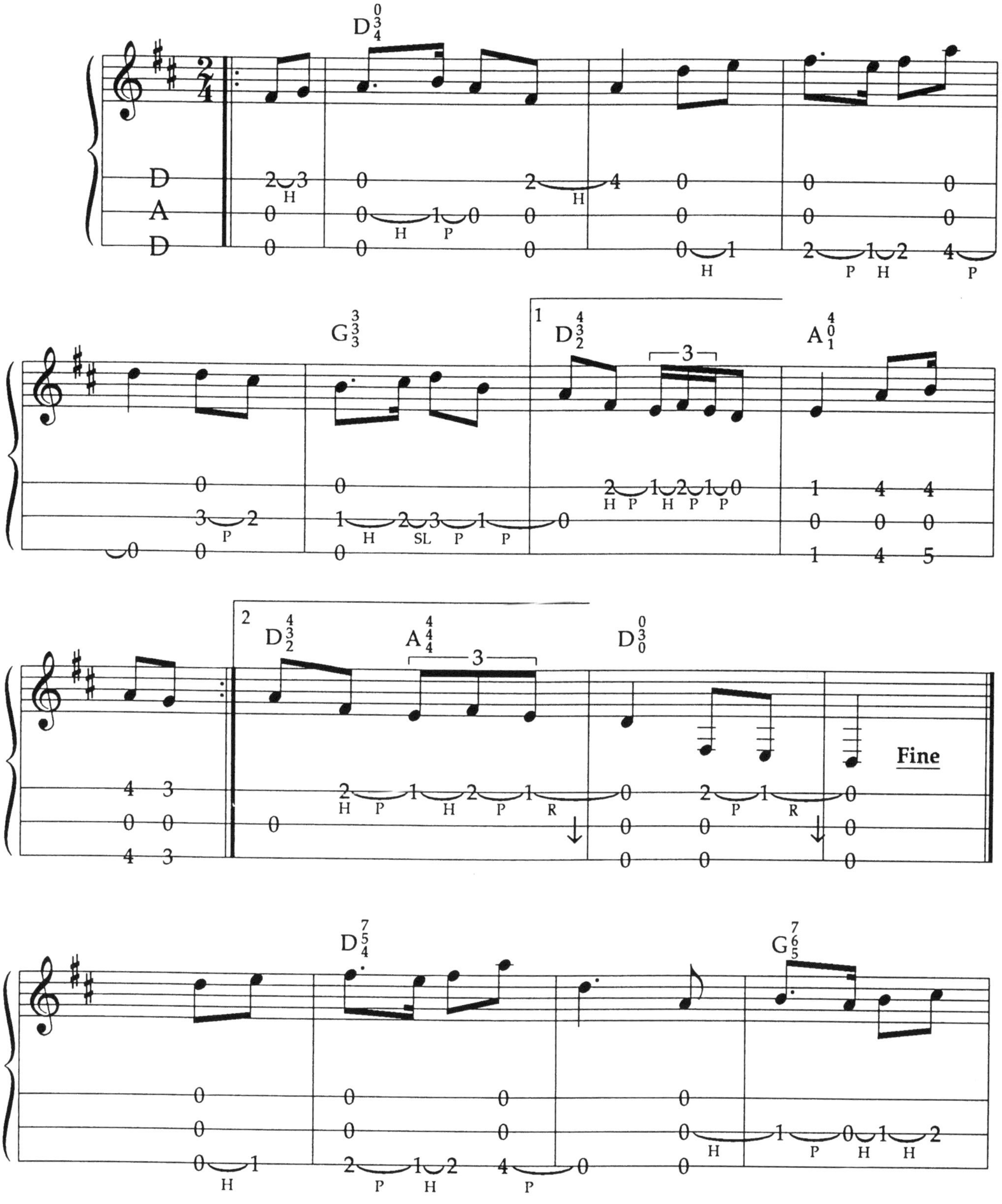

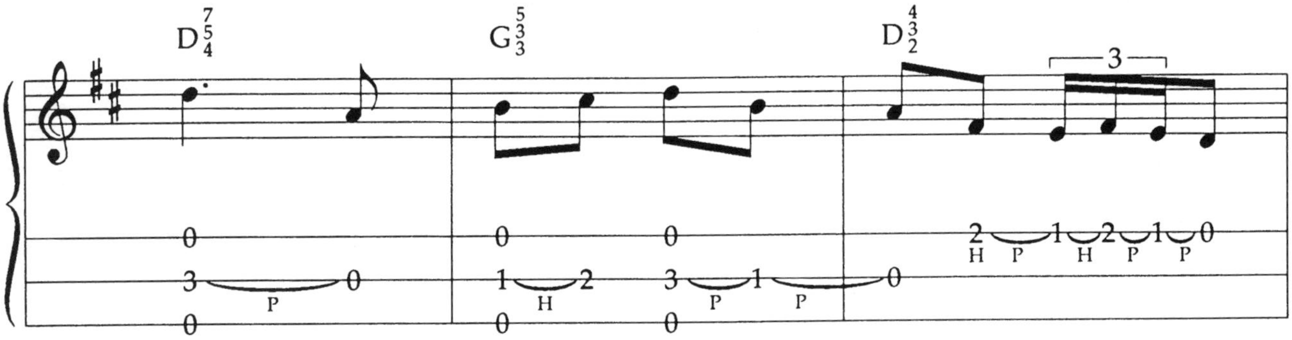

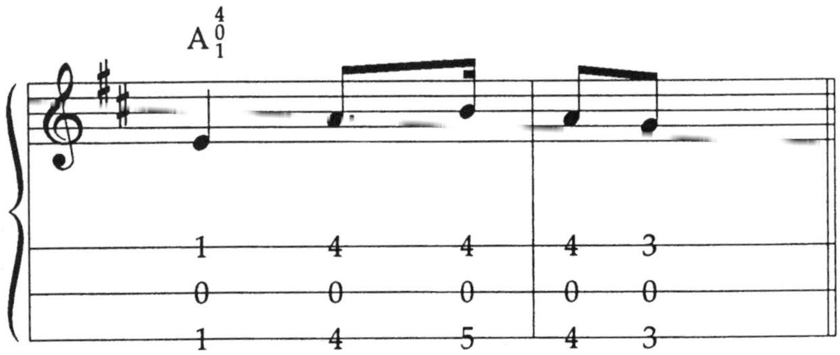

D. C. al Fine

BONAPARTE'S RETREAT

Tune : DD-A-D

Traditional

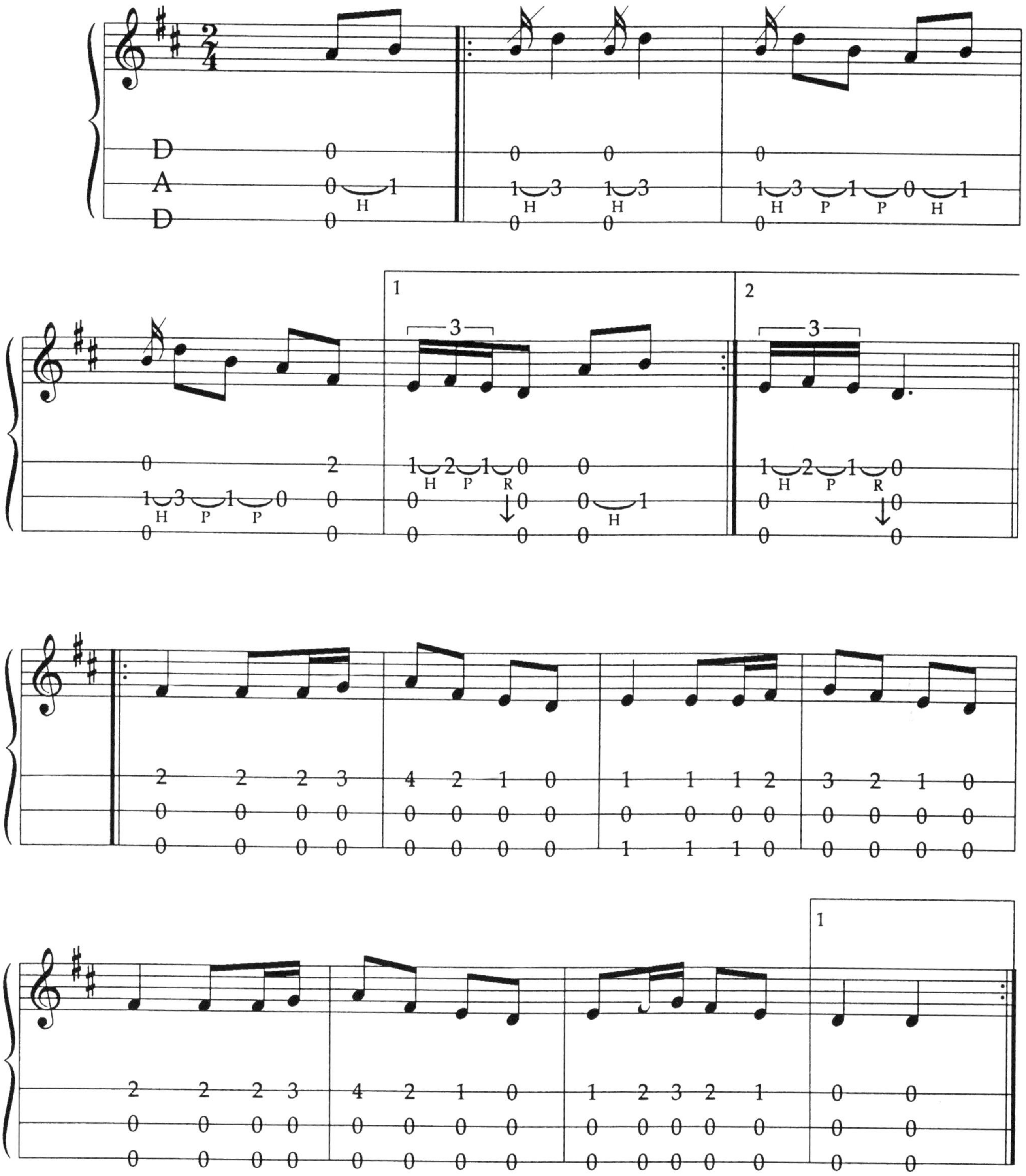

CANARIOS

Tune : DD-A-D

Gaspar Sanz
(1640-1710)

THE CHANTER'S SONG

Tune : DD-A-D

Trad. Irish March

CLUCK OLD HEN

Tune : DD-A-A

Traditional

My old hen's a— good old hen— she lays eggs for the rail- road men.
Some times six and— some times ten— she lays eggs for the rail- road men.
A
A
D
Cluck old hen cluck and squall ain't laid an egg since late last fall.
Cluck old hen cluck and sing ain't laid an egg since late last spring.

THE CUCKOO

Tune : DD-A-D

Traditional English

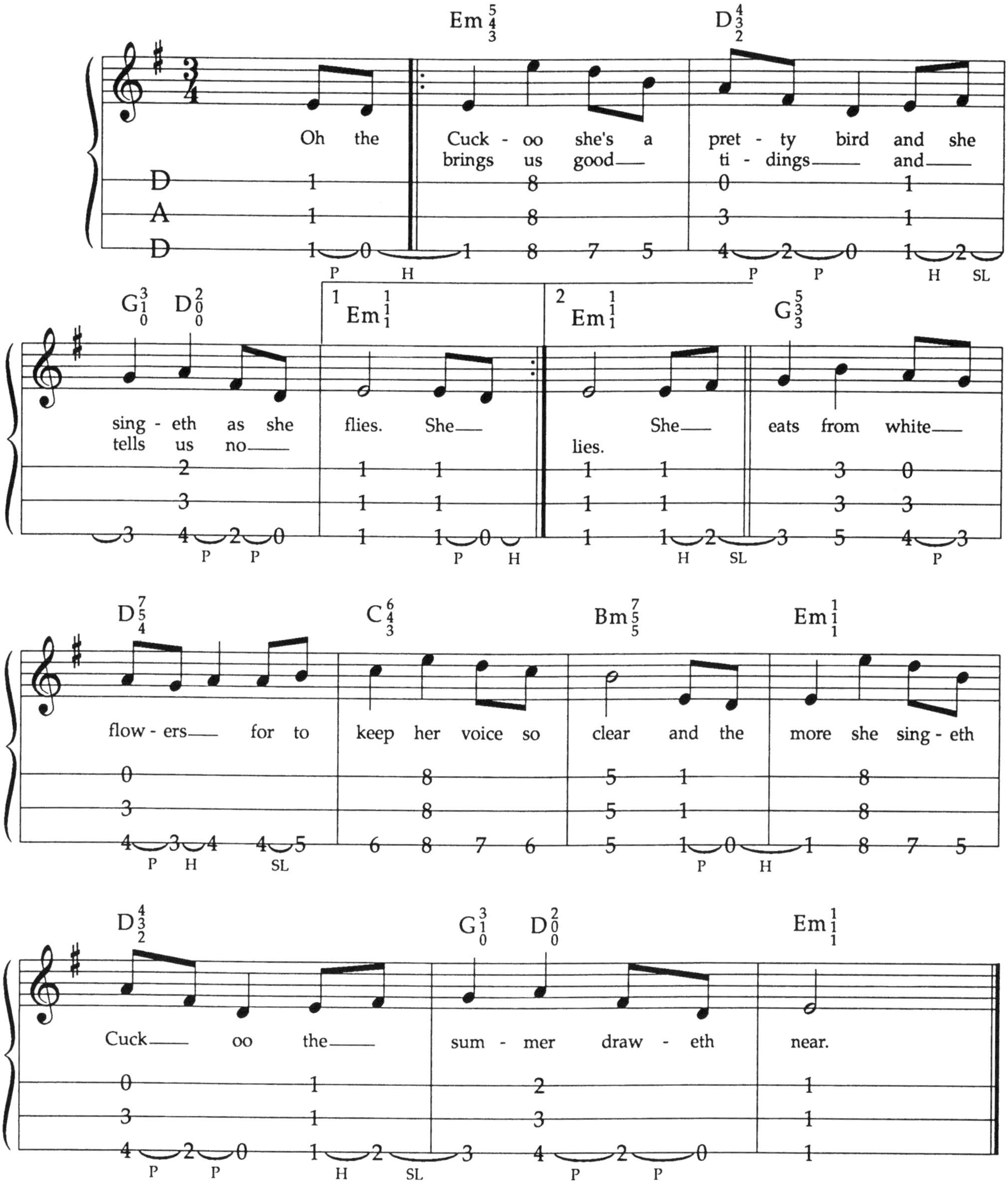

As I was a-walking and a-talking one day
I met my own true love as she passed along that way
Oh, the courting was a pleasure but the parting was a woe
For I found her false-hearted, she would love me and go.

I wish I was a scholar and could handle the pen
I'd write my own true love and to all you roving men
I would warn them of the grief and woe that attended to their lies
I'd wish them to have pity on a flower when it dies.

Come all ye tender maidens and take warning by me
And never place affection upon the willow tree
For the leaves they will wither and the roots they'll soon run dry
My own love has forsaken me and I cannot tell you why.

Repeat first verse.

Cumha Eoghain Rua Ui Neill

Tune : DD-A-D

Turlough O'Carolan
(1670-1738)

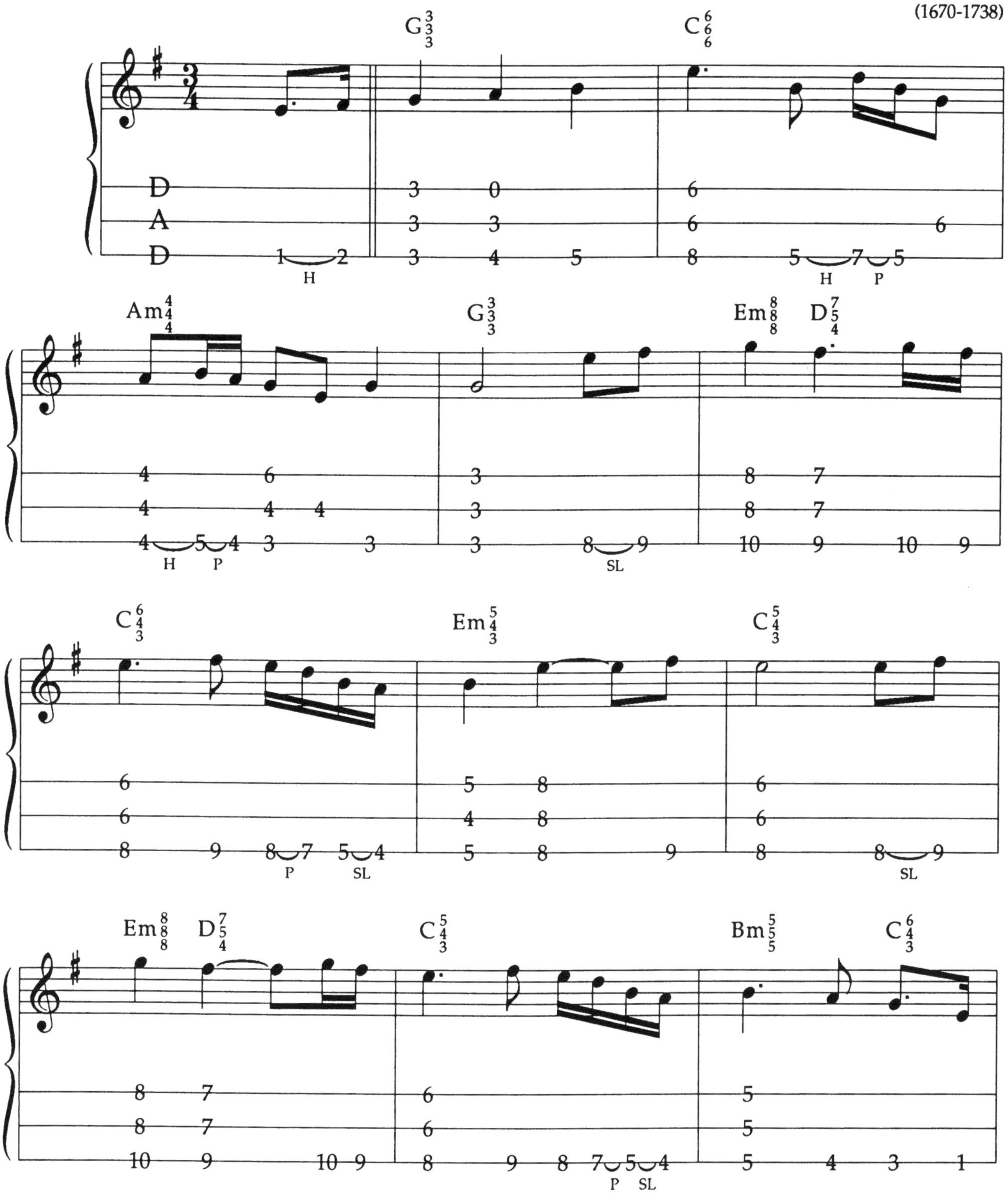

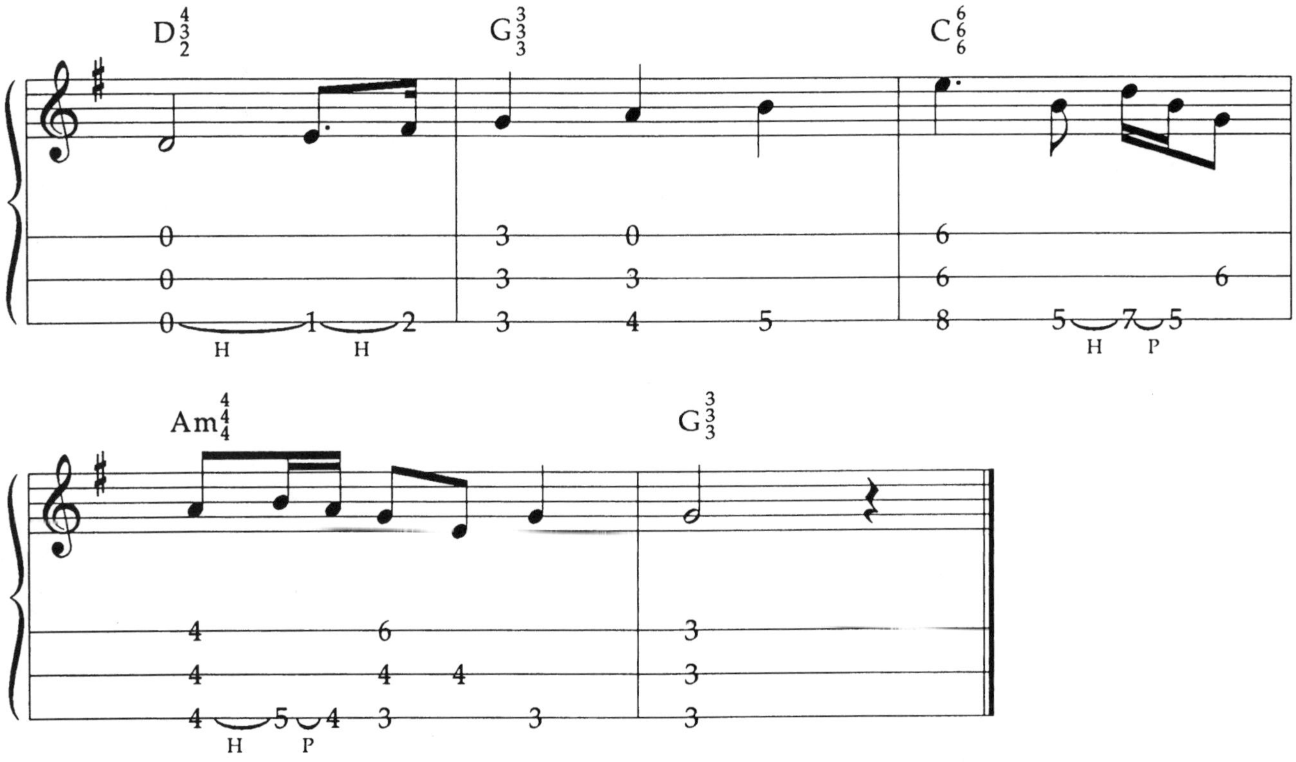
D
G
C
Am
G

THE DARK FOREST

(THE FOREST OF GARTH)

Tune : DD-A-A

Traditional Irish

DOUCE DAME JOLIE

Tune : DD-A-A

Guillaume de Machaut
(1300-1377)

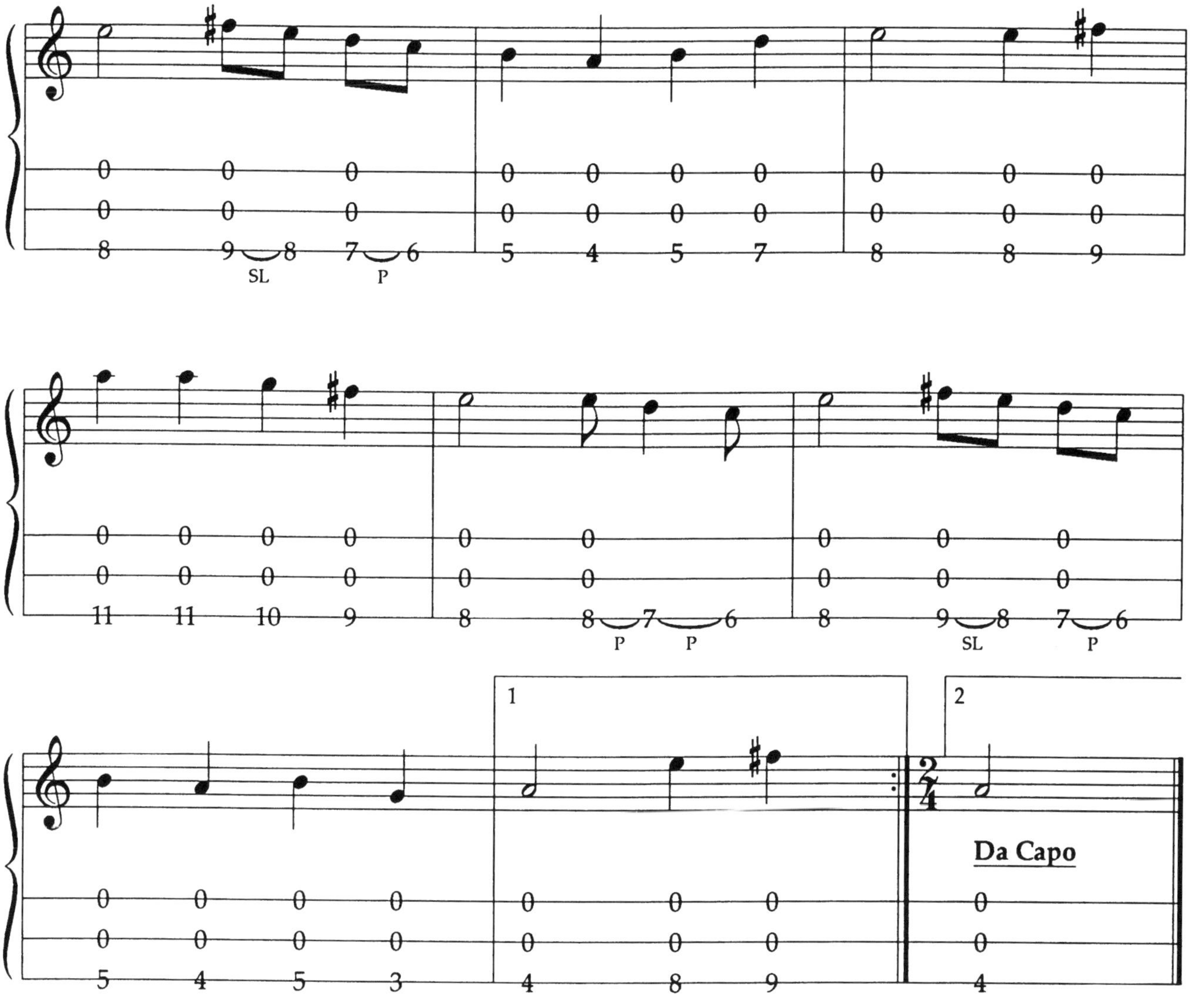
SL
P
1
2
Da Capo

DURANGO

Tune : D-D-G-D

Neal Hellman

C2
G
H P
1
Gsus
G

D7
2,3
C2
GM7
Dsus
rit.
GM7
Dm 9
G6
Bdim
E7
D2
Am11
D7

Gsus
G
CM7
D6
Dsus
D7
C2
rit.
4
Gsus
rit.
G

EL TUTU

Tune : DD-G-D

Traditional Italian

FIDDLIN' BAGPIPES

Tune : DD-A-D*

Traditional American

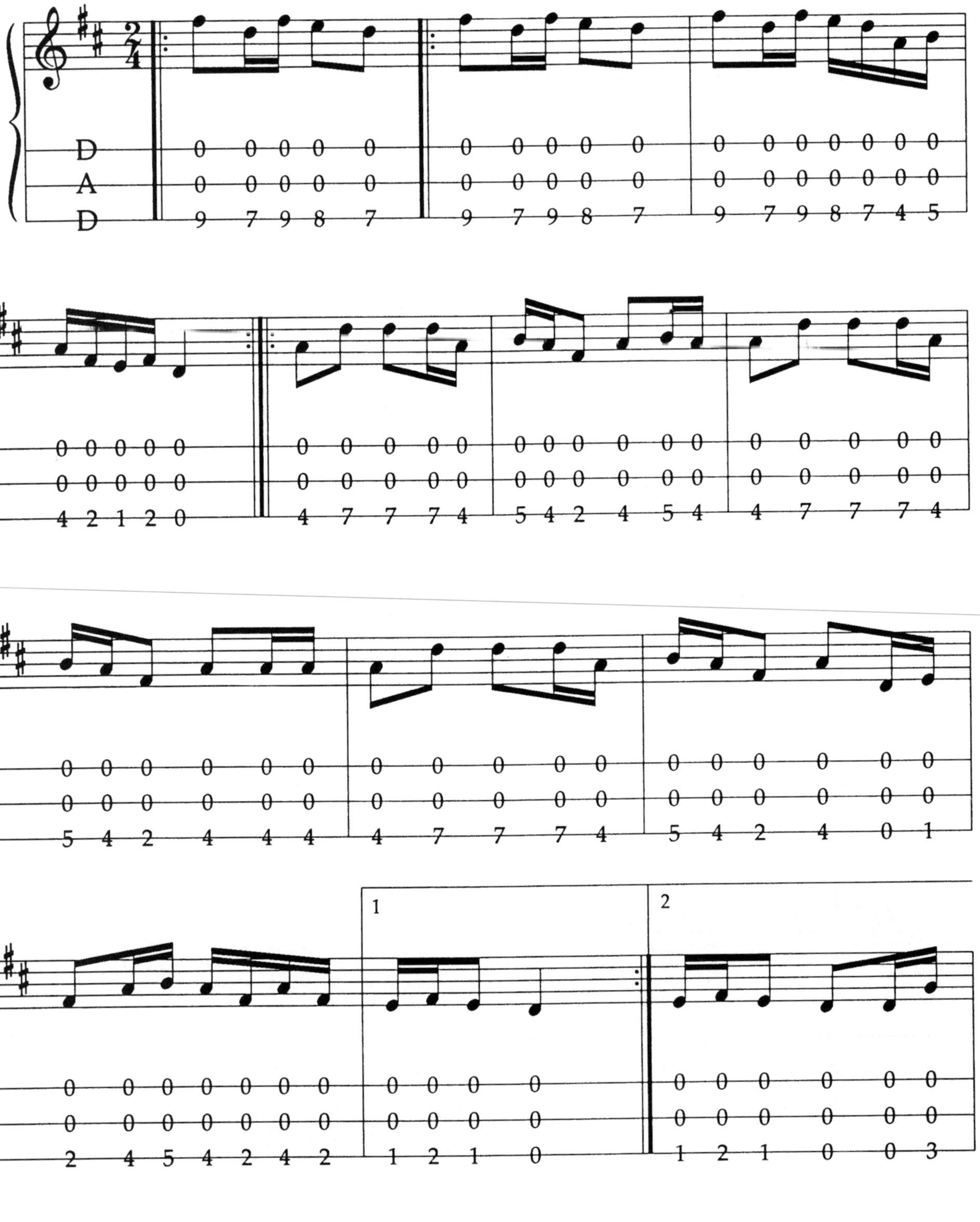

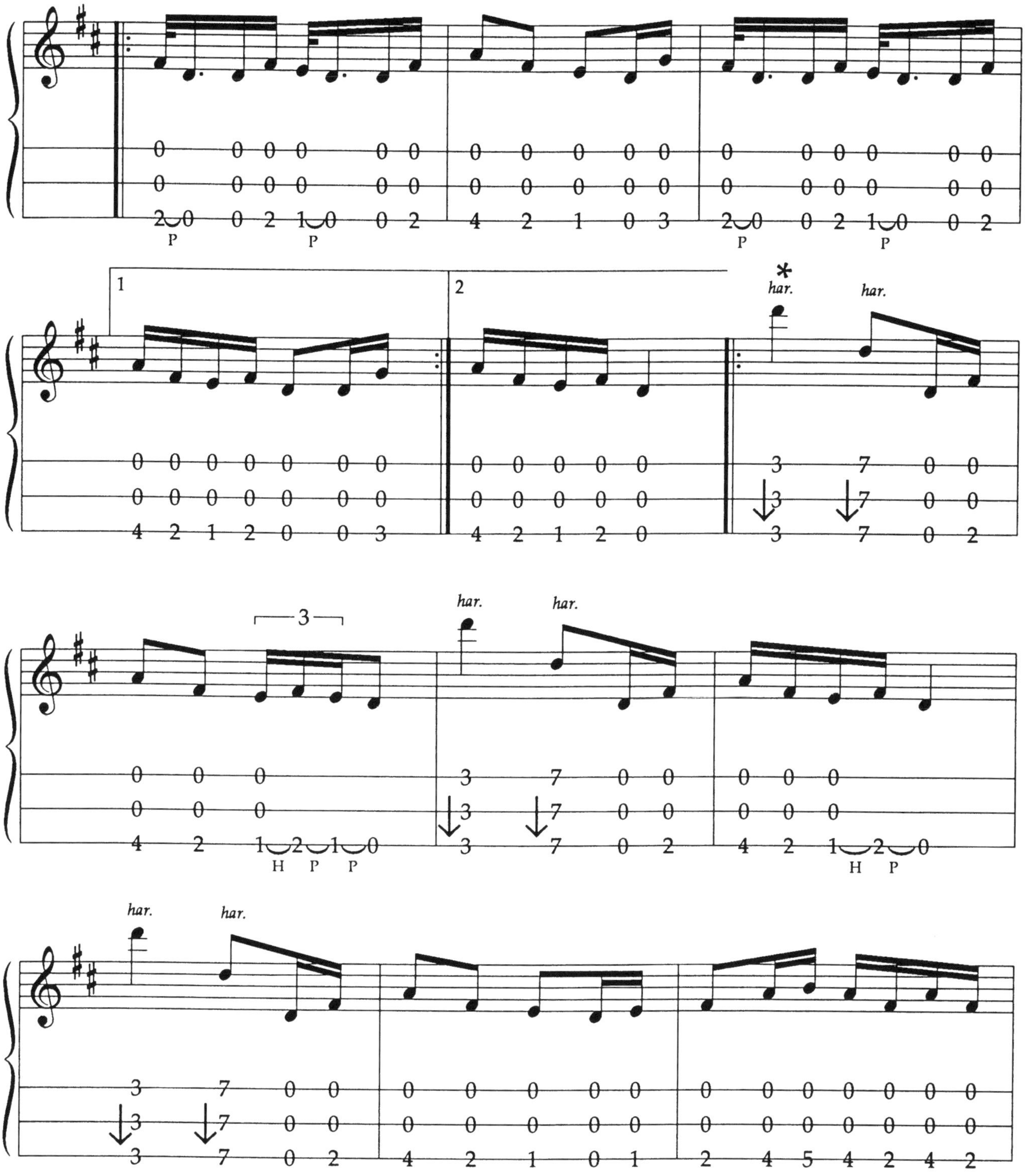

*harmonics across all 3 strings

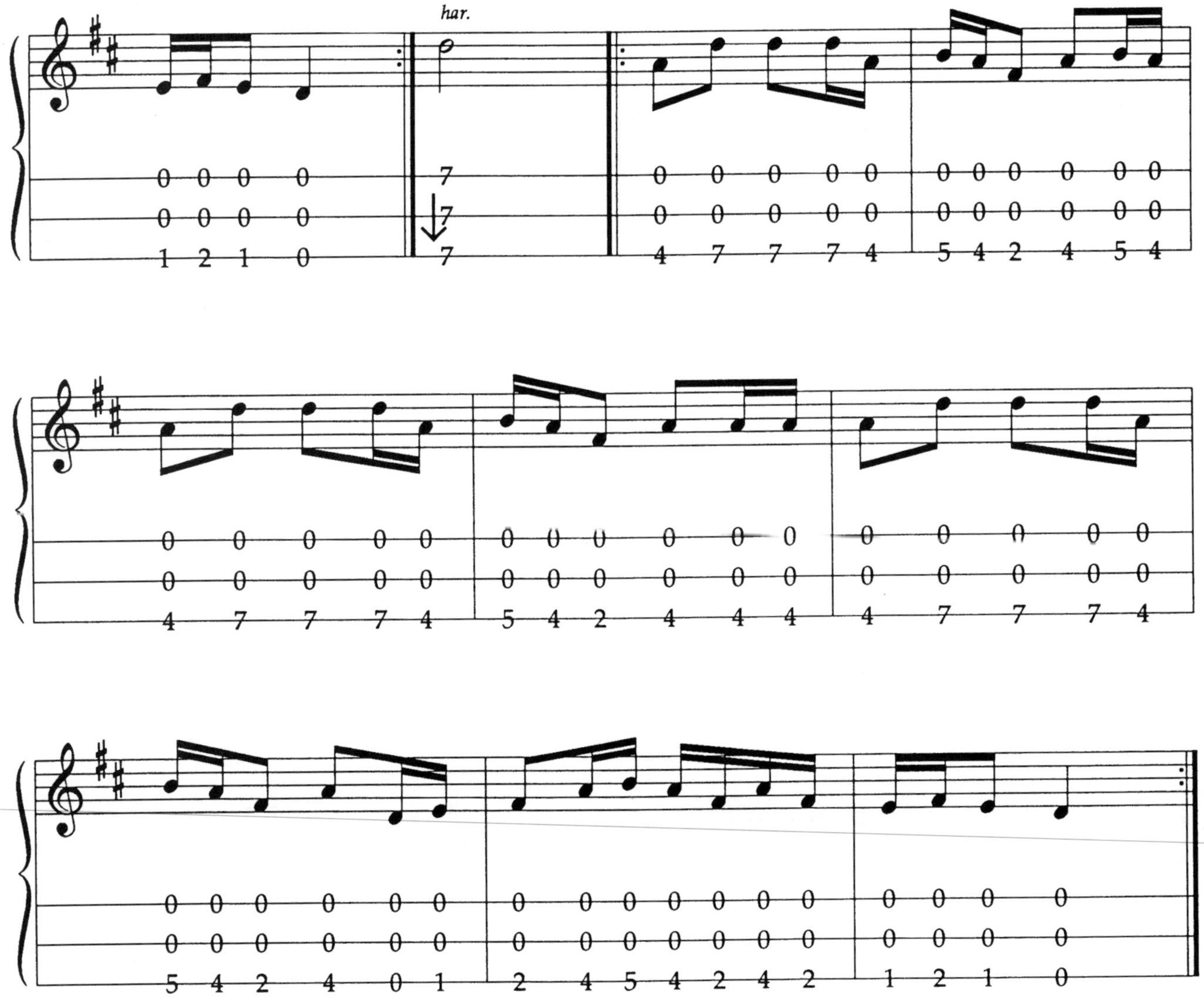
har.

FISHER'S HORNPIPE

Tune : G-D-G

James Fishar

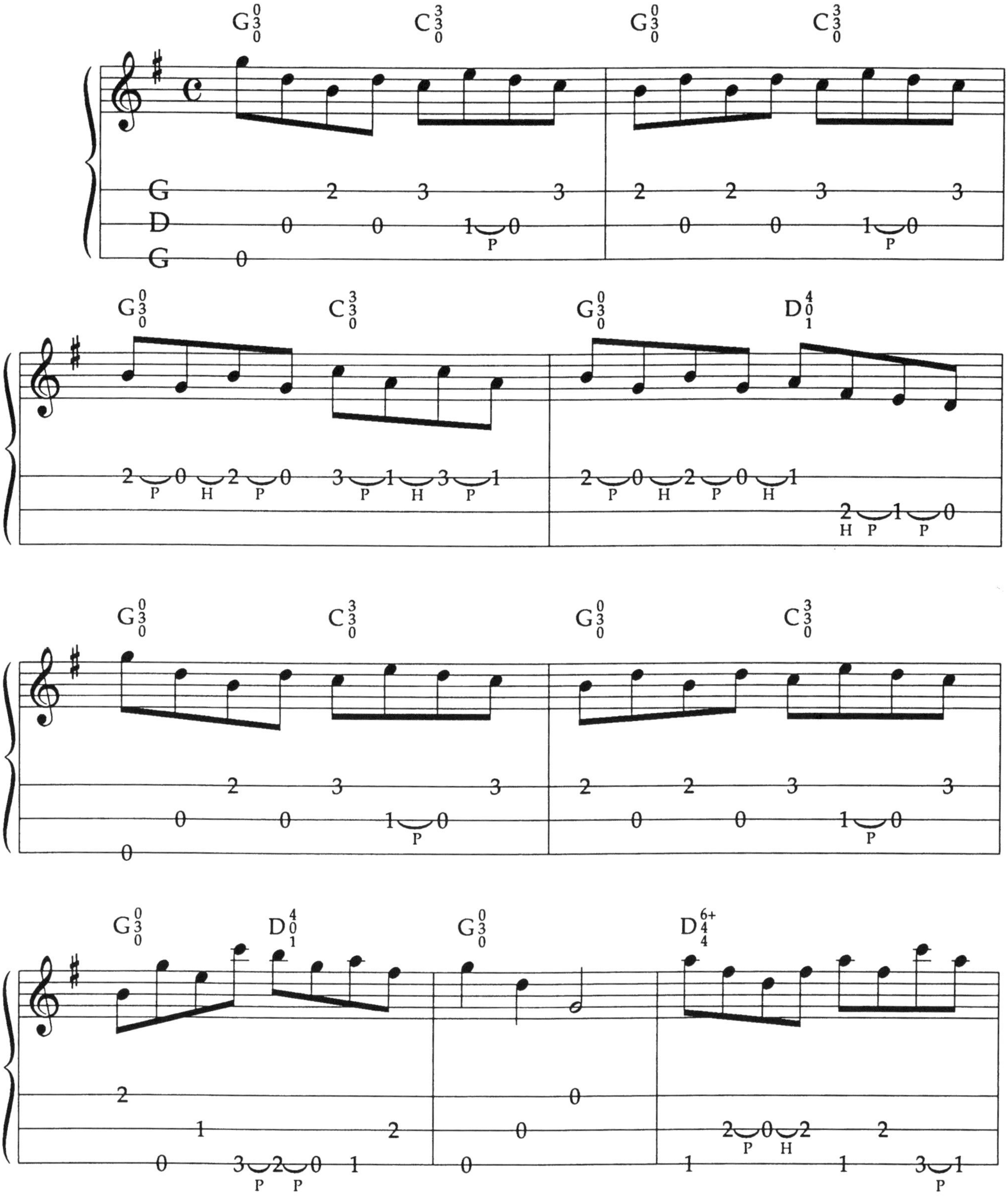

You can, of course, tune the dulcimer DD-A-D and play the same fret numbers. You will now be playing in the key of D.

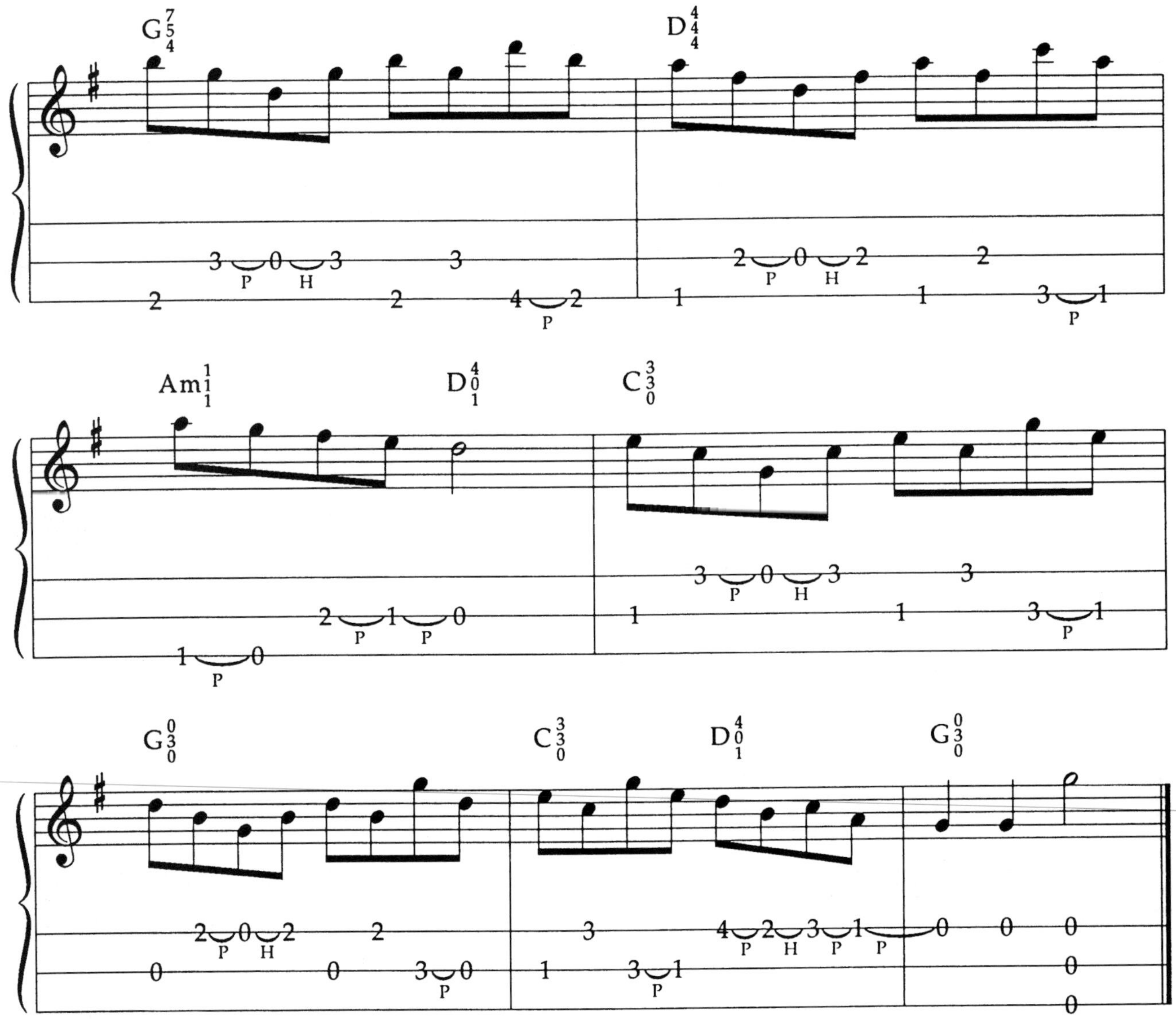
G
D
Am
D
C
G
C
D
G

FOGGY DEW

Tune : DD-A-D

Trad. Irish

GAELIC AIR

Tune : DD-A-D

Traditional Irish

THE GIRL I LEFT BEHIND ME

Tune : DD-A-D

Traditional

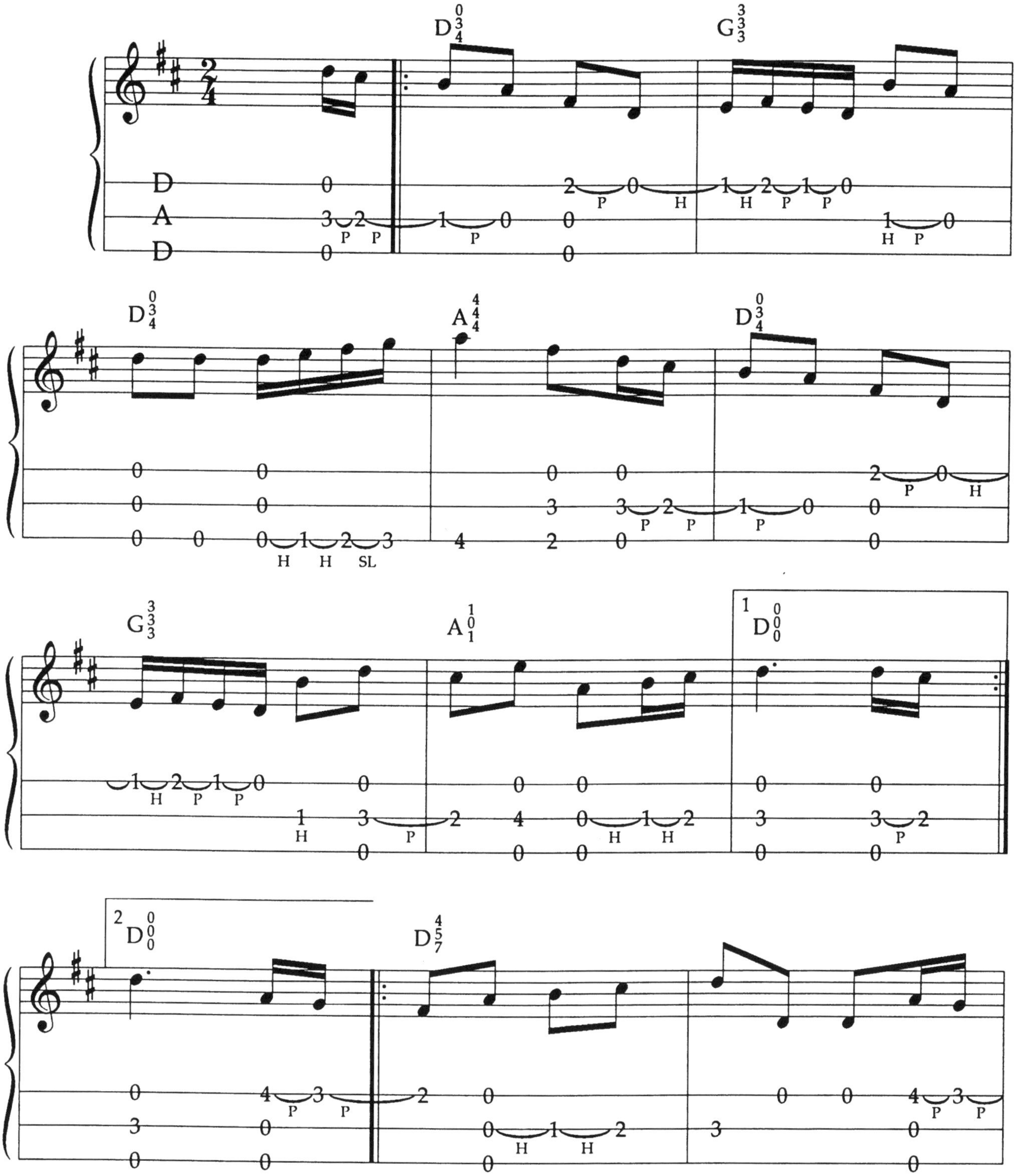

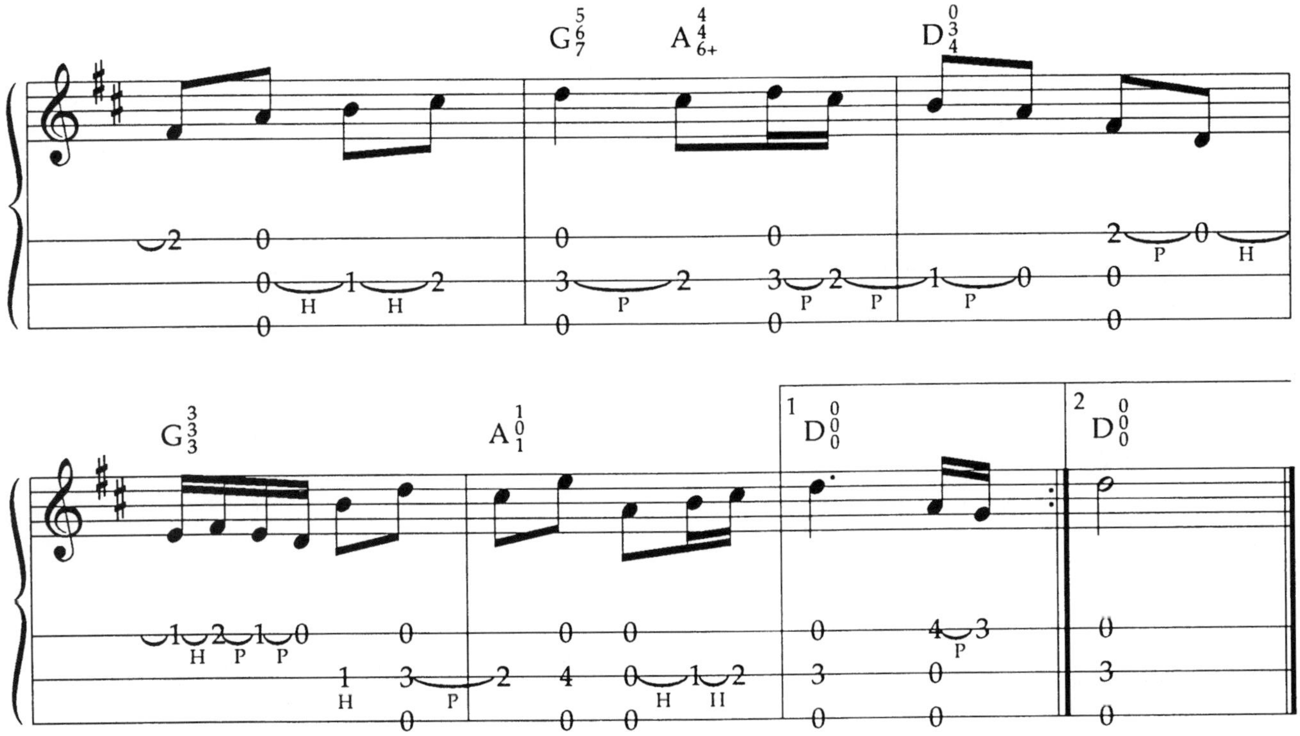
G
A
D
G
A
D
D

GOD REST YE MERRY, GENTLEMEN

Tune : DD-A-D

Traditional

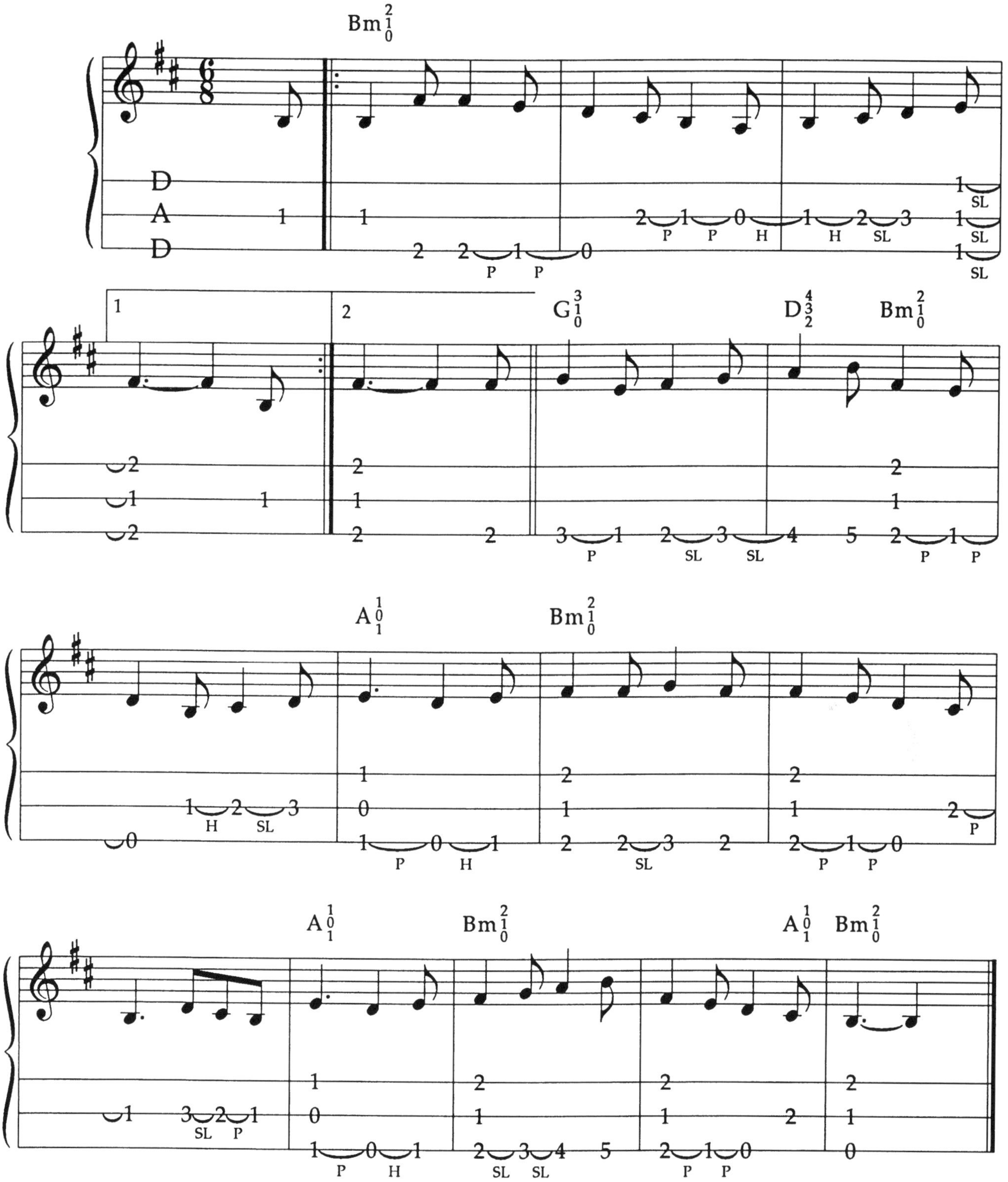

God rest ye merry, gentlemen,
Let nothing you dismay;
Remember Christ our Savior
Was born on Christmas Day;
To save us all from Satan's power
When we were gone astray.

Oh tidings of comfort and joy
Comfort and joy,
Oh tidings of comfort and joy.

'Twas in the town of Bethlehem
This blessed infant lay
They found him in a manger
Where oxen feed on hay;
His mother Mary kneeling
Unto the Lord did pray.

Oh, tidings of comfort and joy,
Comfort and joy,
Oh, tidings of comfort and joy.

Now to the Lord sing praises,
All you within this place;
And with true love and brotherhood
Each other now embrace;
God bless your friends and kindred
That live both far and near,

And God send you a happy New Year!
Happy New Year!
And God send you a happy New Year!

HEWLETT

Tune : DD-A-D

Turlough O'Carolan
(1670-1738)

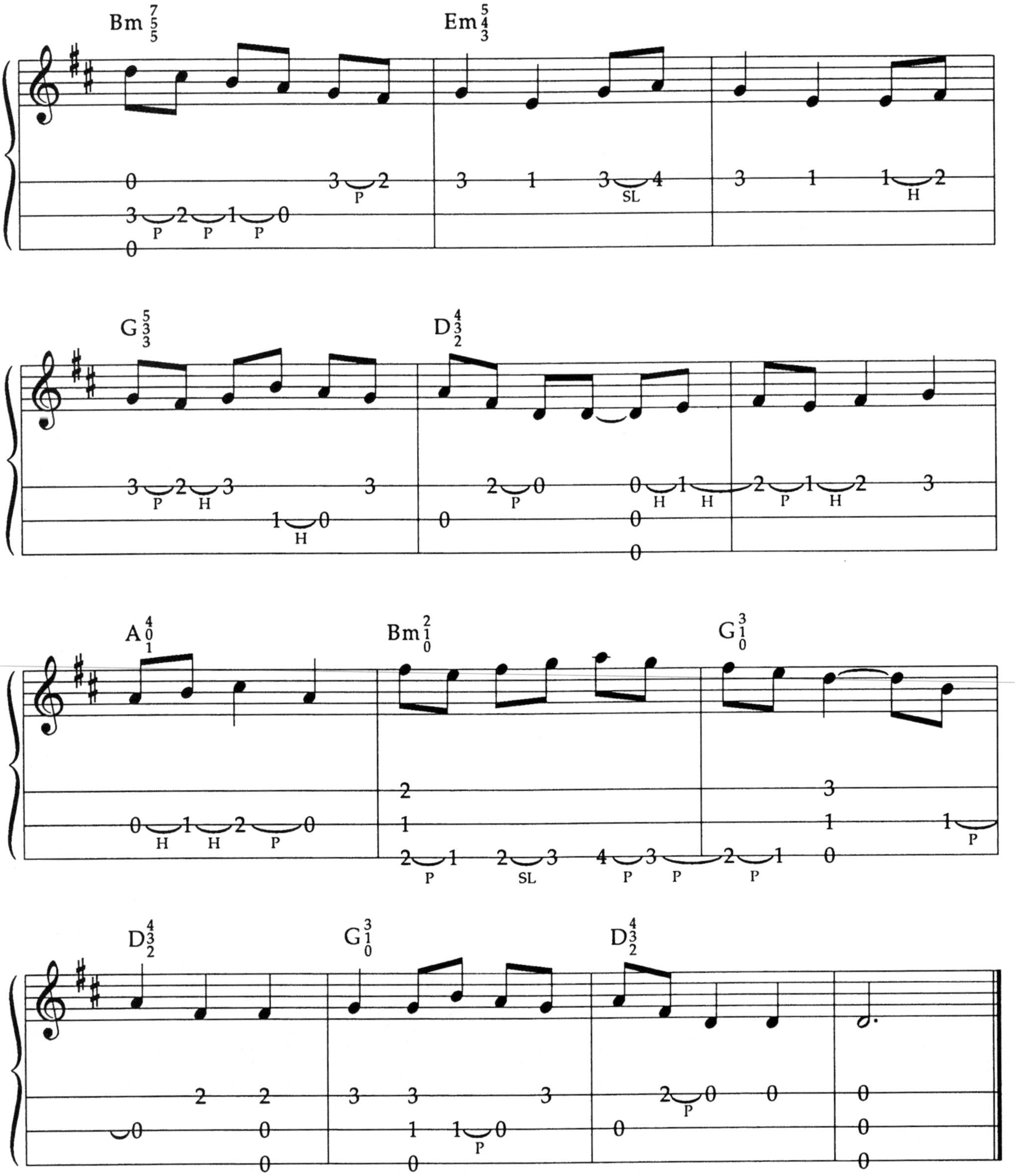
Bm
Em
G
D
A
Bm
G
D
G
D

I AM A LITTLE SCHOLAR

Tune : Bb-F-C

Traditional

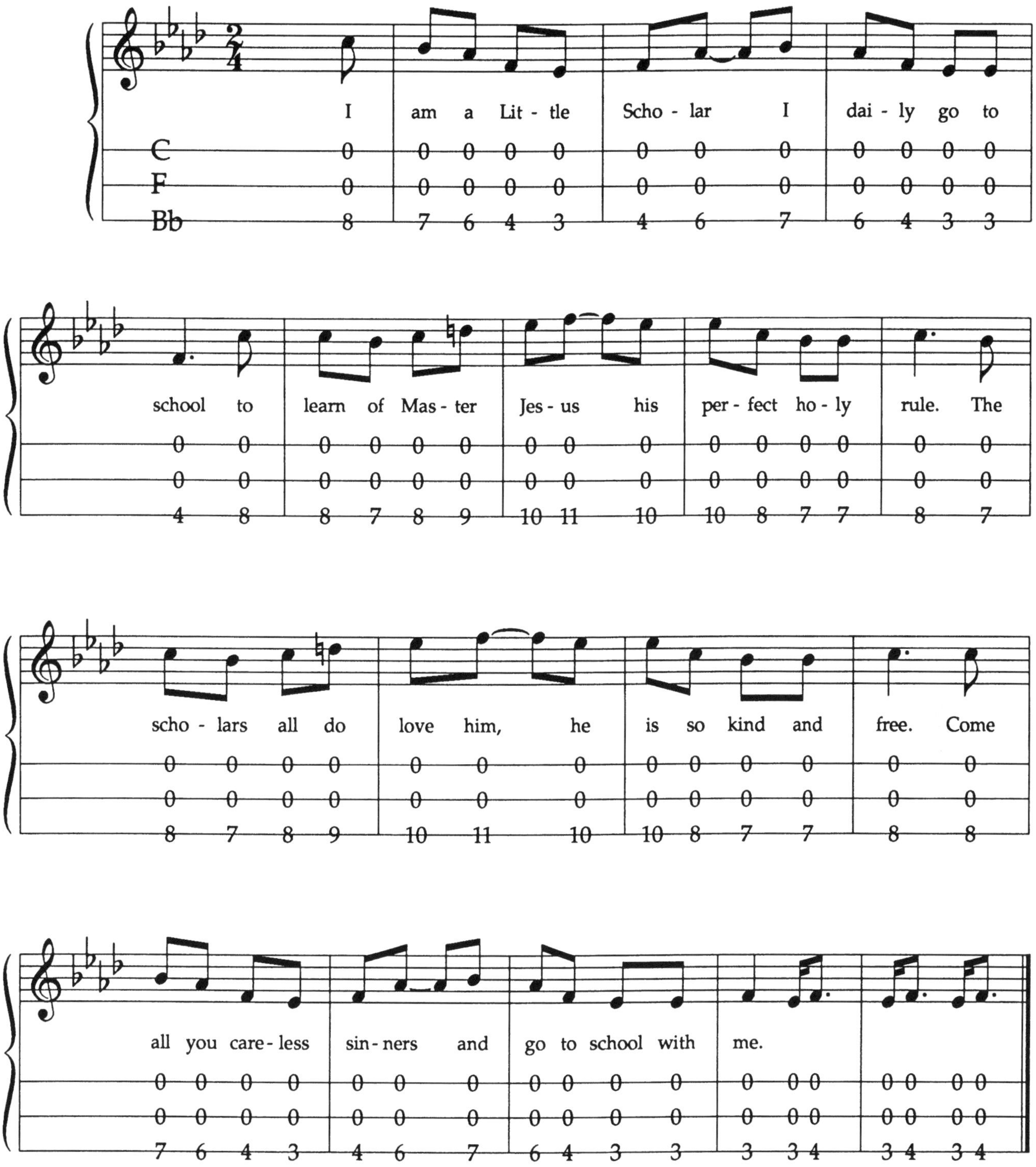

I am a little Christian
The Lord hath made me so
All over a new creature
What wonders he can do
I love the things I hated
I hate the things I loved
My master is preparing me
To reign with him above.

I am a little preacher
I preach the gospel free
Whatever my master gives me
I give it all away
And when my heart is empty
I go to the master's store
He smiles with love upon me
And gives me all the more

I am a little poet
I wrote this little song
And oft times it doth cheer me
When I am all alone
And if there is another
Who would wish to learn the same
I pray the Lord to set their souls
All in a heavenly flame.

I am a little scholar
I daily go to school
To learn of master Jesus
His perfect holy rule
The scholars all do love Him
He is so kind and free
Come all you careless sinners
And go to school with me.

I'VE BEEN ALL AROUND THIS WORLD

Tune : DD-A-D

Traditional

Verse 1:
Upon the Blue Ridge Mountains
There I'll take my stand
Upon the Blue Ridge Mountains
There I'll take my stand
With a pistol in my pocket
And a rifle in my hands
I've been all around this world.

Verse 2:
Lulu O Lulu, come open up the the door
Lulu O Lulu, won't you open up that door
Before I have to blow it down
With my old .44
I've been all around this world.

Repeat Chorus

Verse 3:
All around Cape Girardeau and half of Arkansas
All around Cape Girardeau and half of Arkansas
O I went so damn hungry I could hide behind a straw
I've been all around this world.

Verse 4:
Put the rope around my neck, hang me up so high
Put the rope around my neck, hang me up so high
The last words that I heard them say
"It won't be long 'til he dies!"
I've been all around this world.

Repeat Chorus

KINGDOM COMING

Tune : DD-A-D

H. C. Work

LA MORT DE COUCY

Dedicated to Barbara W. Tuchman

Tune : DD-A-D

Neal Hellman

D
A
G
Bm
G
Bm
D
Em
A
ritard

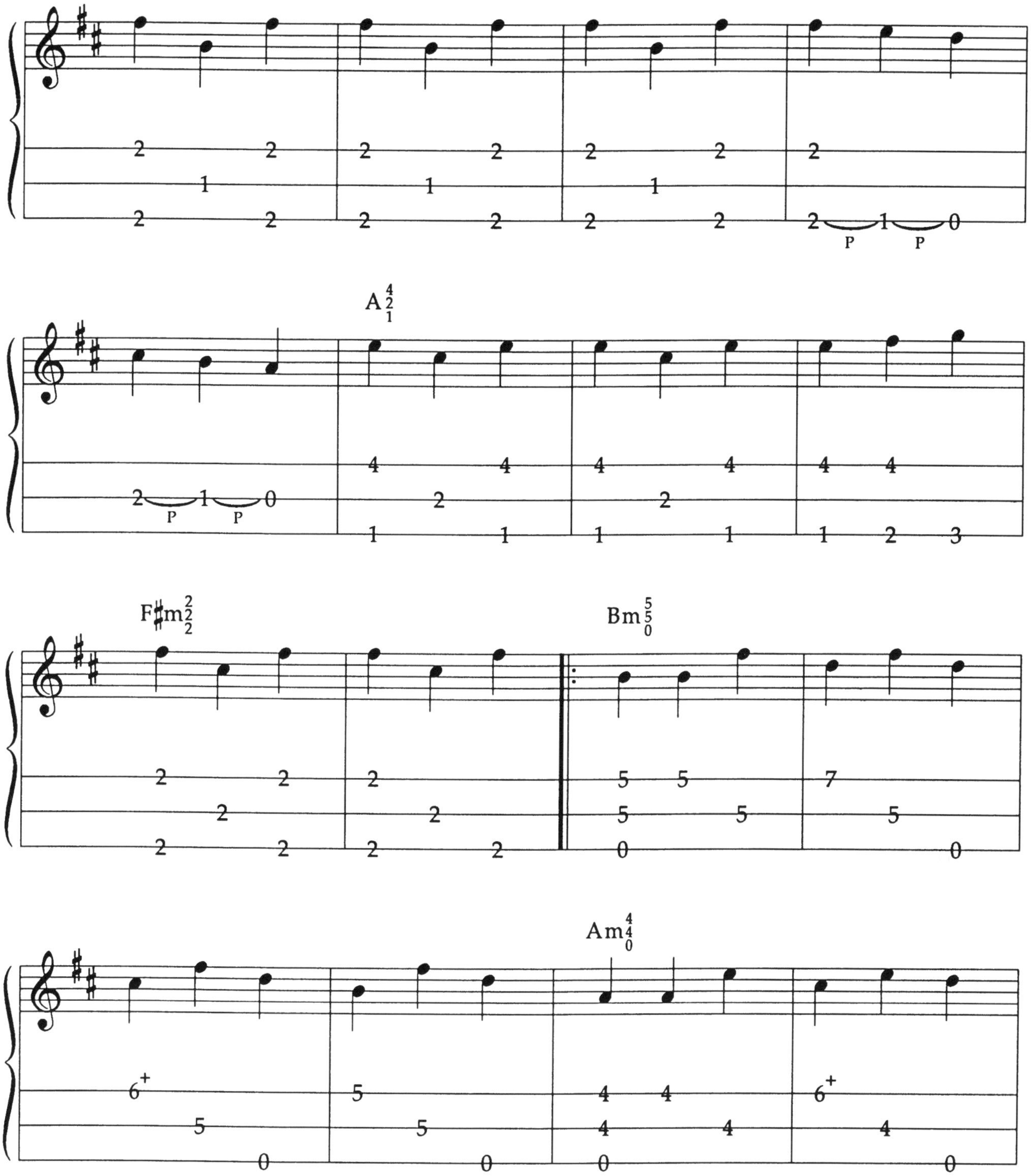
A
F♯m
Bm
Am

G
D
G
D
F♯m
A
ritard
Bm

The French knight Enguerrand de Coucy VII led a remarkable life when the world seemed ready to perish. In Europe in the 14th century, the Black Plague had killed one third of the known world's population. England and France were involved in a war that would last for 100 years. Roving armies owing allegiance to no one were ravaging Europe. Strikes and mass peasant uprisings were common occurrences. Like a great storm from the east, the Ottoman Turks invaded, following the Danube and setting up an outpost just 300 miles from the Black Sea.

It was a time of incredible terror and despair. The rye flour was struck with a fungus that would cause entire villages to have mass hallucinatory experiences — the phenomenon called St. Anthony's Fire. People would dance in circles till they saw visions of demons or Christ and then would "all fall down." Seeking salvation, the Flagellants travelled from town to town mortifying their flesh for all horrified onlookers to see. Secret societies and cults of death were not uncommon. A split in the Papacy, with one Pope in Rome the other in Avignon, caused people to question the very basis of their faith and fear for their eternal fate.

One of the most glorious and powerful of all the French knights, Enguerrand de Coucy VII inherited the largest fortress in Europe. Located to the northeast of Paris, it guarded the King from the English campaigning out of the port of Calais. Coucy's titles were many: Grand Bouteiller of France, Count of Soissons, Grand Marshall of France, General, Councillor and ambassador for the French Kings. He was acquainted with the great men of his day, including the historian Froissart and the poet Chaucer, author of *The Canterbury Tales*.

Coucy campaigned all over Europe and Northern Africa (see map below). At Nicopolis on September 26, 1396, his prudent orders were ignored by the glory-hungry European knights. The crusade failed and Coucy was taken prisoner along with other nobles, and marched back to Brusa.

Coucy died in captivity before the ransom money came. His death may have been from wounds or illness ... or perhaps it was the grief of tasting defeat for the first time in a great career; and of sensing the fall of the final curtain on an age he knew all too well.

All the preceding information as well as inspiration for *La Mort de Coucy* is from the wonderful book **A Distant Mirror** by Barbara W. Tuchman (Alfred A. Knopf Publications, New York, 1978).
Map: Elise Huffman

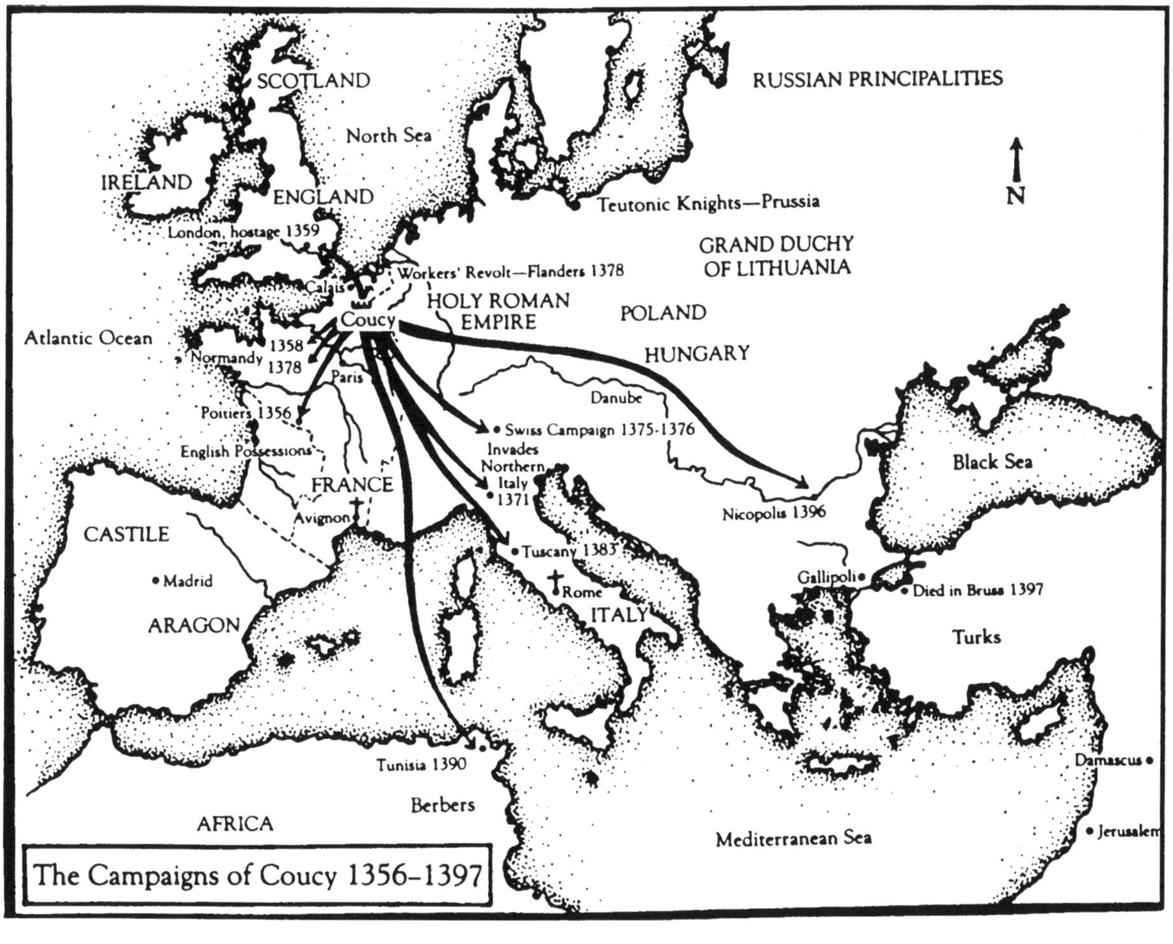

THE LAKES OF PONTCHARTRAIN

Tune : DD-A-D

Traditional Irish

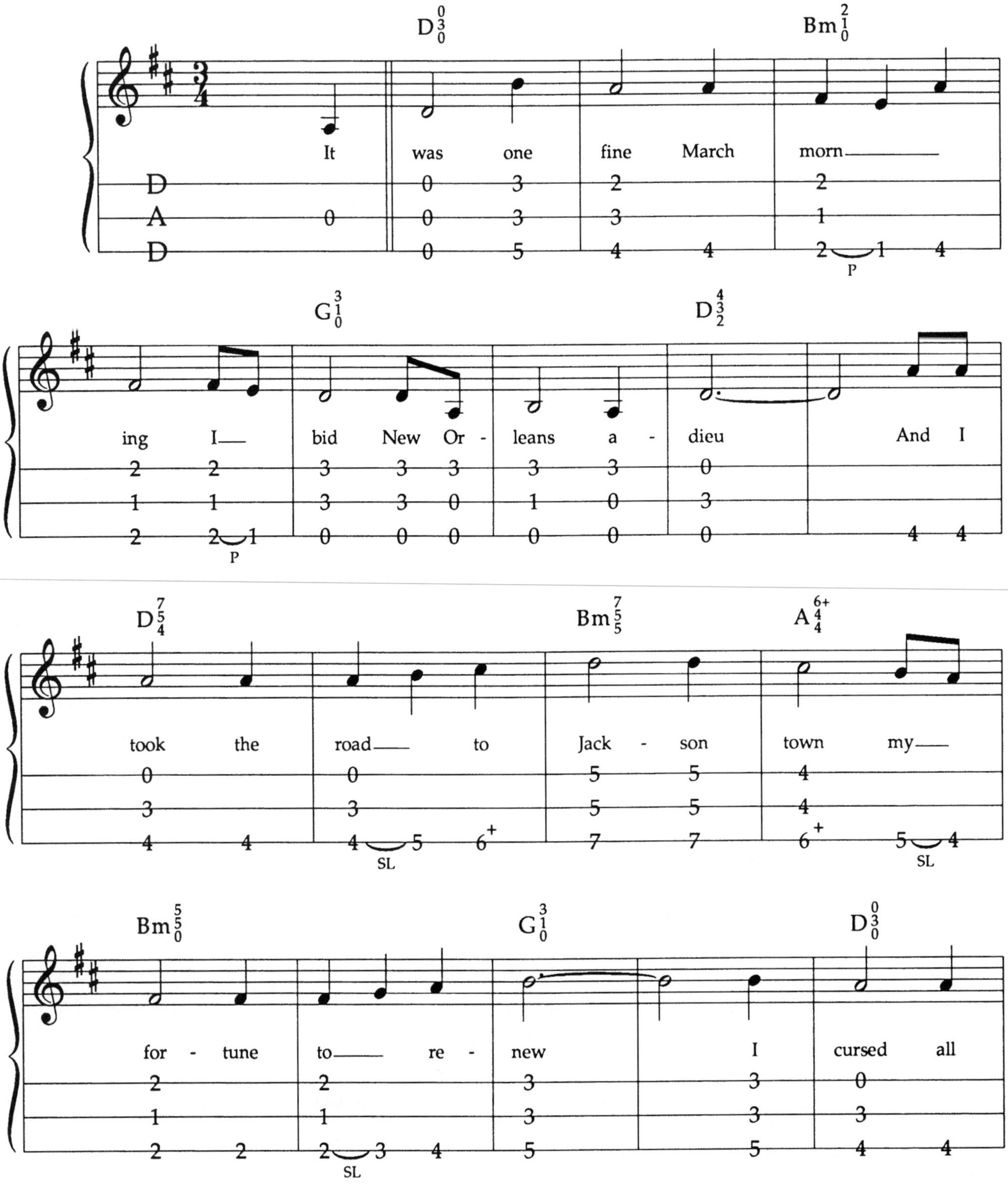

Bm A Bm
for— eign mon - ey no— cred - it could— I
G D Bm
gain which filled my heart with long— ing
G D
for the— Lakes of Pont - char - train.

I stepped on board a railroad car
Beneath the morning sun
And I rode the rods till evening
Then I laid me down again
All strangers there no friends to me
Till a dark girl towards me came
And I fell in love with a Creole girl
On the Lakes of Ponchartrain.

I said "Me pretty Creole girl
My money here' s no good
If it weren't for the alligators
I'd sleep out in the woods."
"You're welcome here kind stranger
Our house is very plain
But we never turn a stranger out
On the Lakes of Ponchartrain."

She took me into her mammy's house
And treated me right well
The hair upon her shoulder
In jet black ringlets fell
To try and paint her beauty
I'm sure would be in vain
So well, so well my Creole girl
On the Lakes of Ponchartrain.

I asked her would she marry me
She said that ne'er could be
For she had brought a lover
And he was far at sea
She said that she would wait for him
And true she would remain
Till he returned to his Creole girl
On the banks of Ponchartrain.

So fare you well my bonny old girl
I'll ne'er may see you no more
I'll ne'er forget your kindness
In the cottage by the shore
And at every social gathering
A flowing glass I'll drain
And I'll drink a health to the Creole girl
On the Lakes of Ponchartrain.

LAUDA

Tune : DD-A-D

Traditional Italian

LAUDA DI MARIA MADDALENNA

Tune : DD-A-D

Traditional Italian

G D D A D A
D Bm F♯m G F♯m
Bm G D Bm
G Em A Bm

LITTLE ST. ANNE

Tune : DD-A-D

Hellman-Weed

Bm D Bm F♯m Bm
F♯m A D G D
Bm G D
Bm G

A E A Bm
G D A Bm D Bm
F♯m Bm F♯m A D G D

LOCH LAVAN CASTLE

Tune : DD-A-D

Traditional Irish

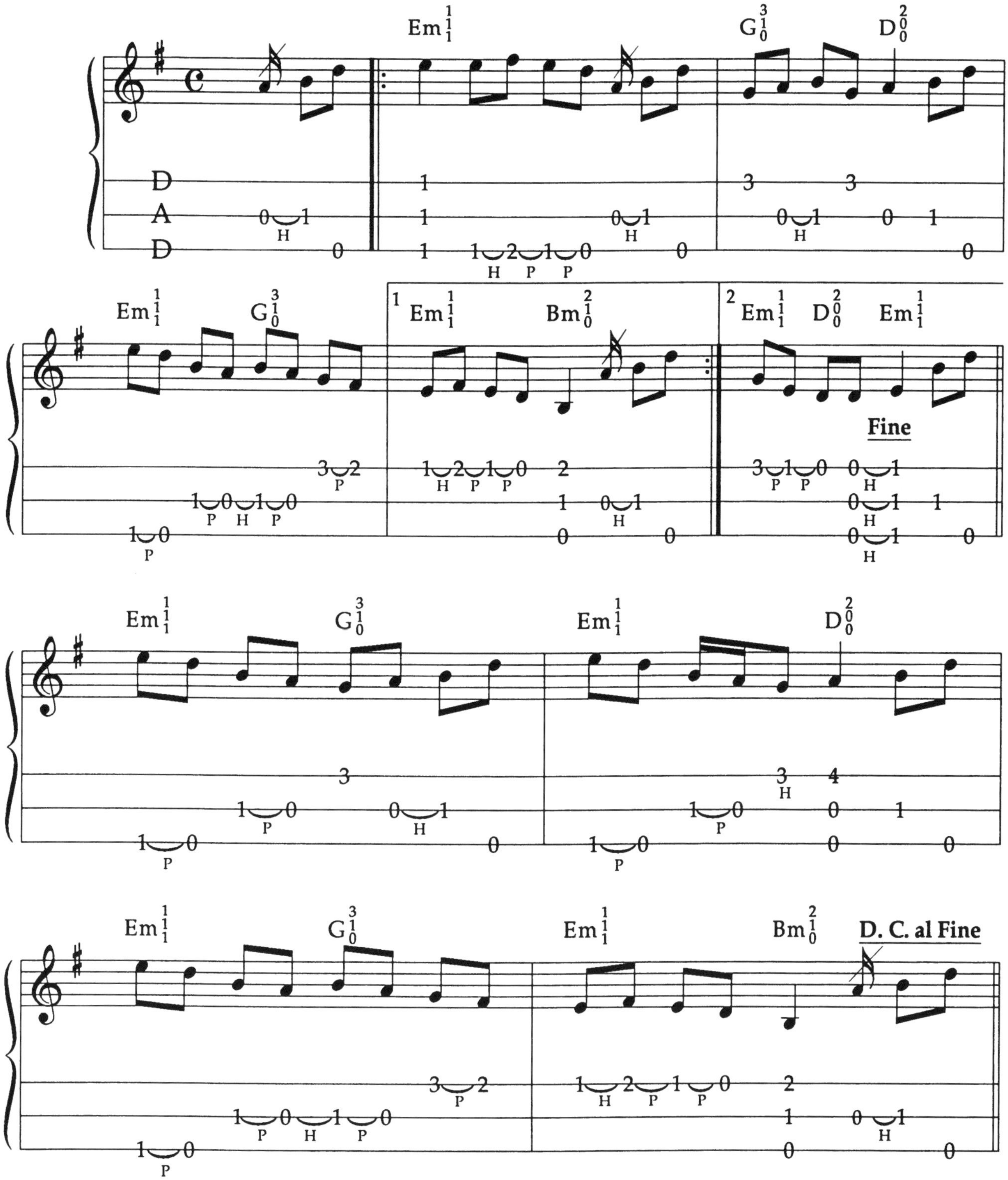

LORD FRANKLIN

Tune : D-D-G-D

Traditional English

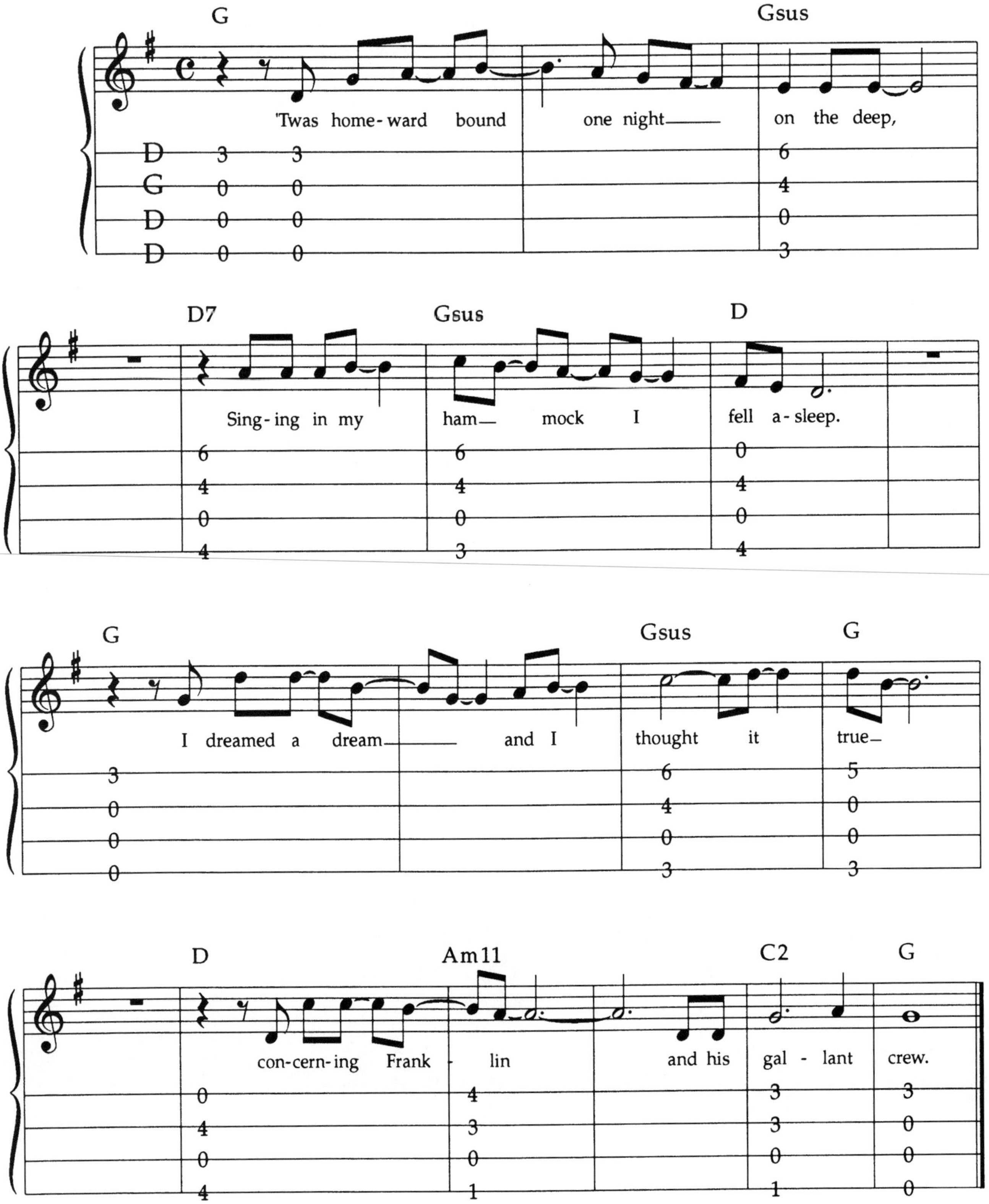

With a hundred seamen he sailed away,
Through the frozen ocean in the month of May
To seek a passage around the pole
Where we poor sailors do sometimes go.

Through cruel hardships they mainly strove,
Their ship on mountains of ice was drove
Only the eskimo in his skin canoe
Was the only one who ever came through

In Baffin's Bay where the whale fish blow,
The fate of Franklin no man may know
The fate of Franklin no tongue can tell
Lord Franklin with his sailors does dwell.

And now my burden it gives me pain,
To find my Franklin I'd cross the Main
Ten thousand pounds, oh, I'd freely give
To say on earth my Franklin did live.

MINUET

Tune : DD-A-D

J. S. Bach
(1685-1750)

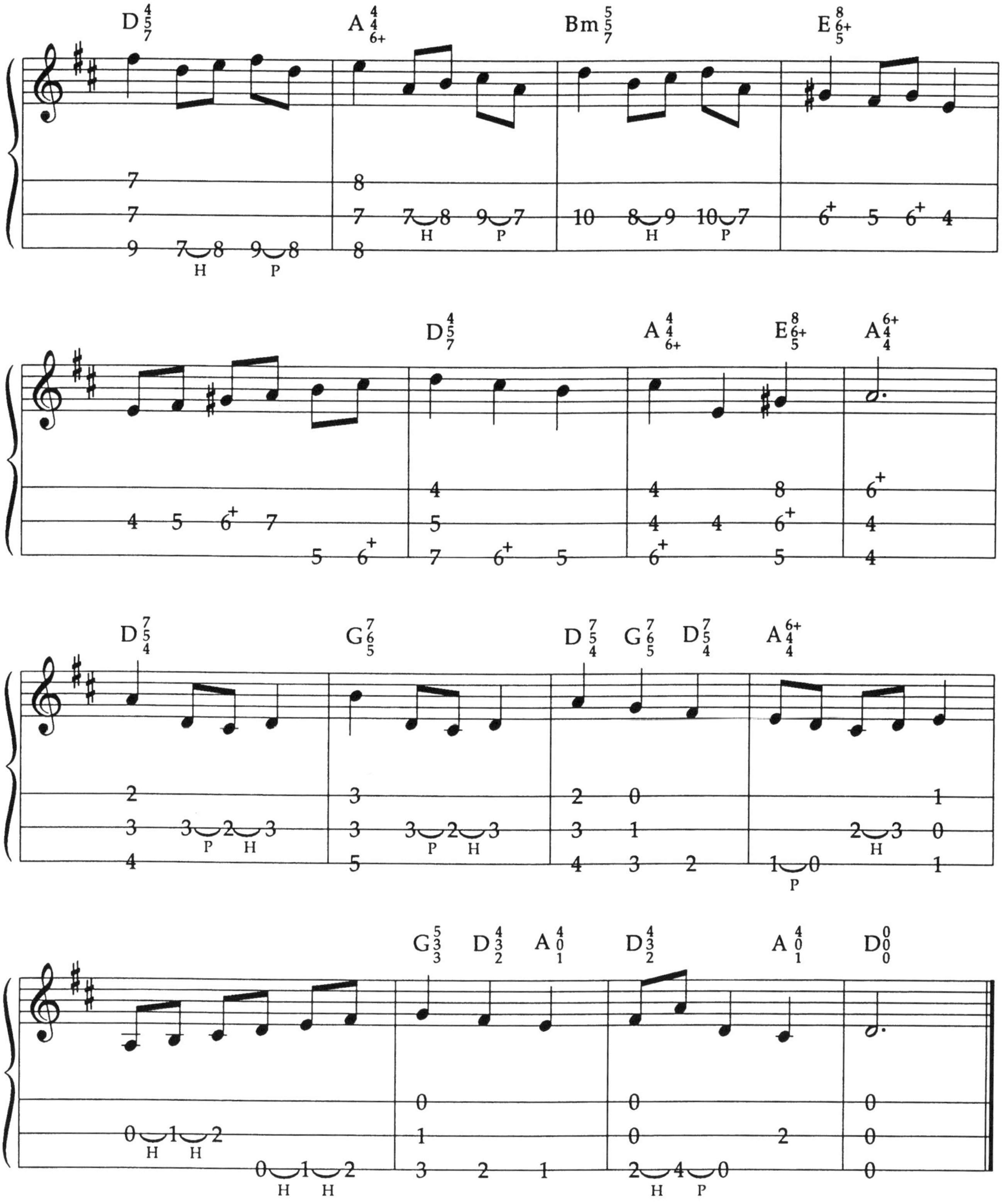
D A Bm E
D A E A
D G D G D A
G D A D A D

MORRISON'S JIG

Tune : DD-A-D

Traditional Irish

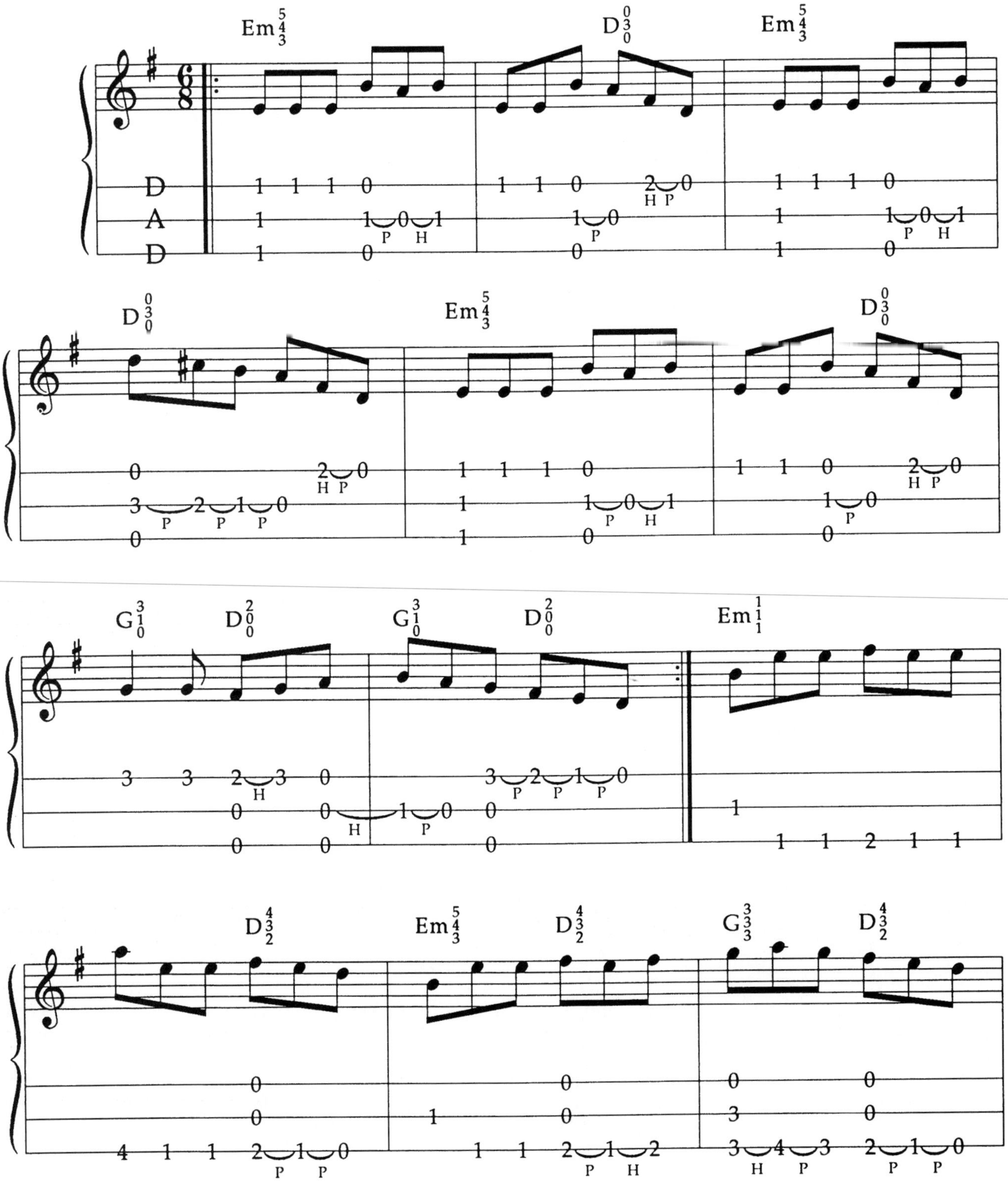

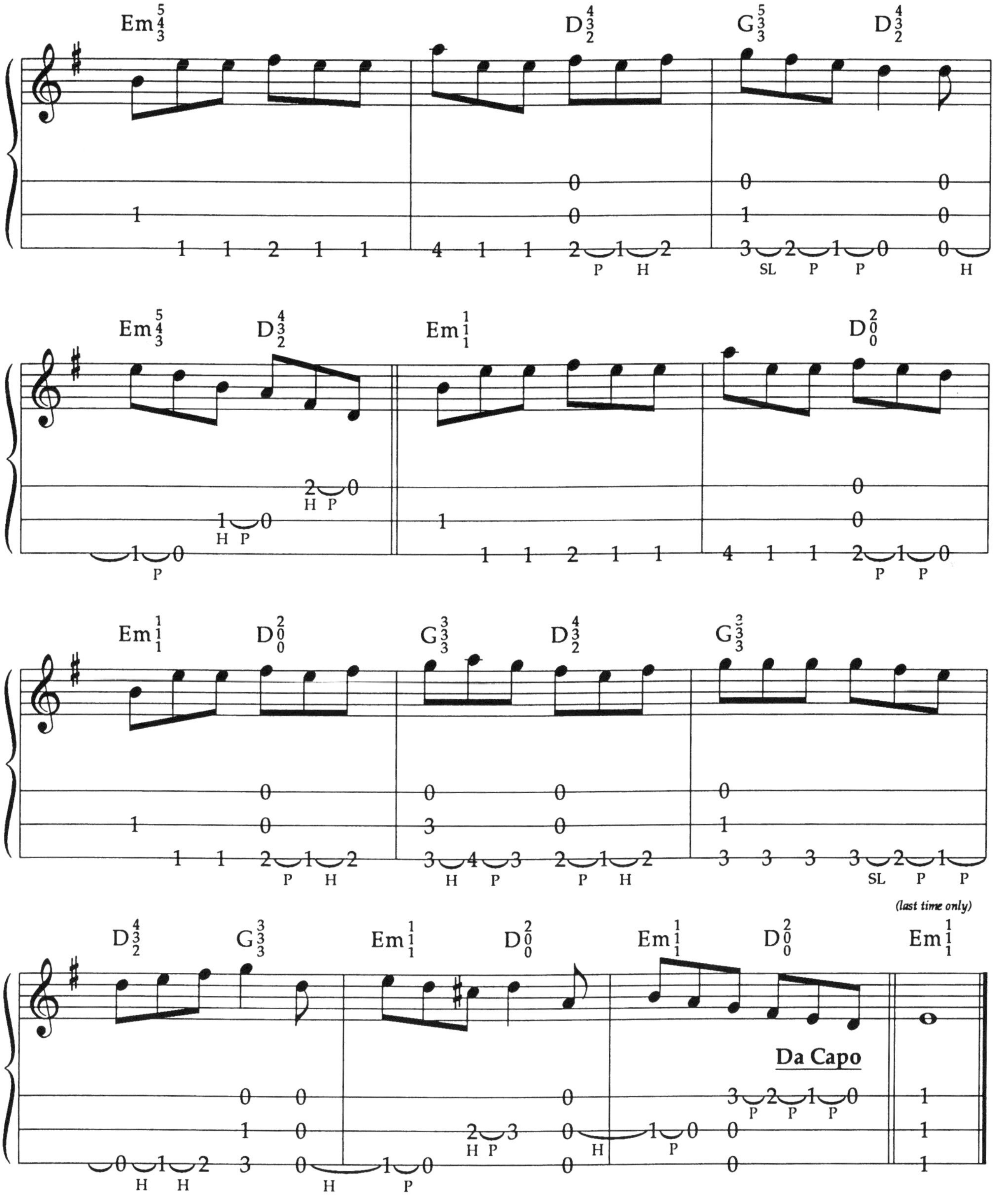
Em D G D
Em D Em D
Em D G D G
(last time only)
D G Em D Em D Em
Da Capo

NEAL'S MAGGOT

Tune : DD-A-D

Traditional Irish

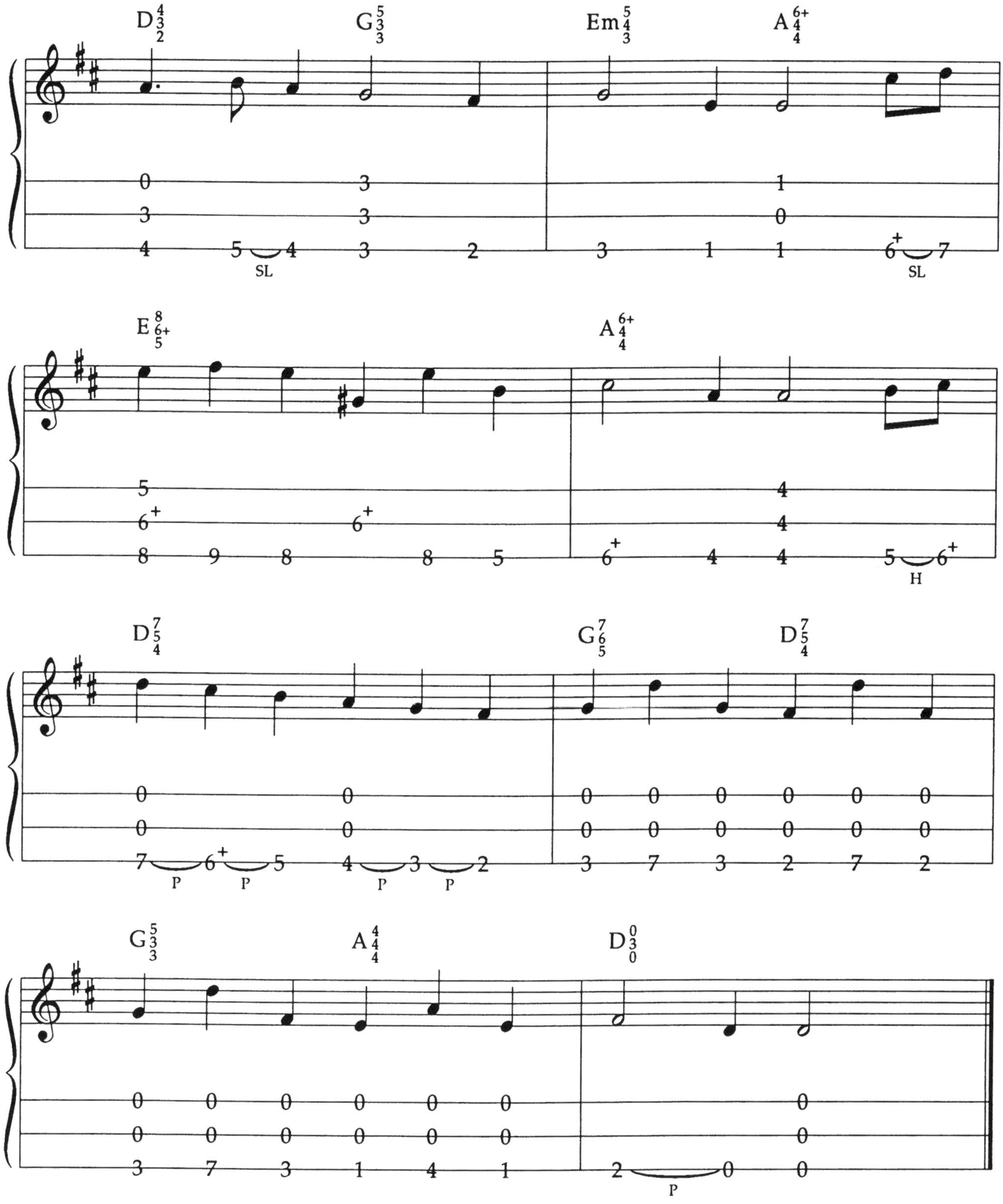
D G Em A
SL SL
E A
H
D G D
P P P P
G A D
P

NINETY-POUND CATFISH

Tune : DD-A-D

Neal Hellman

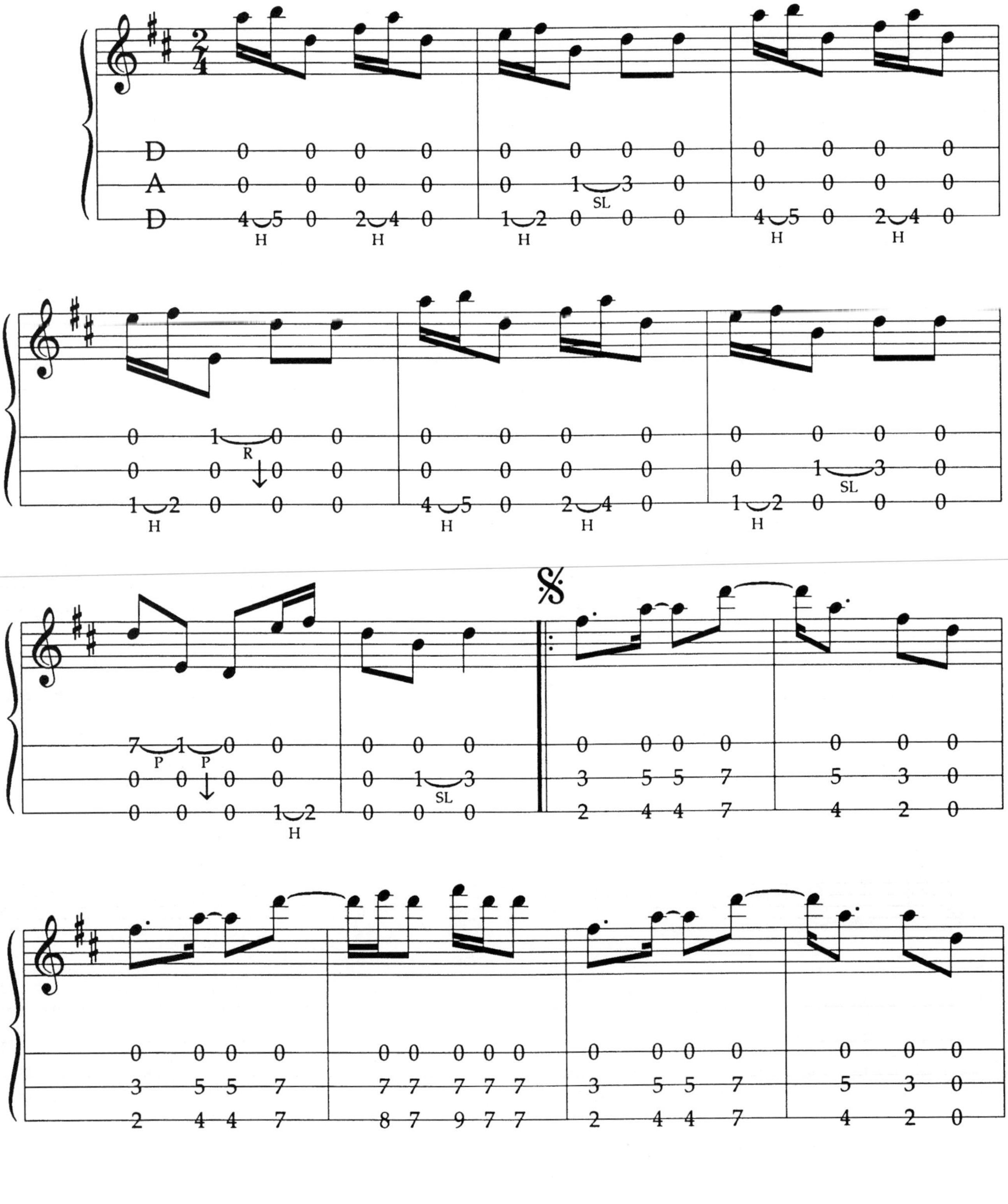

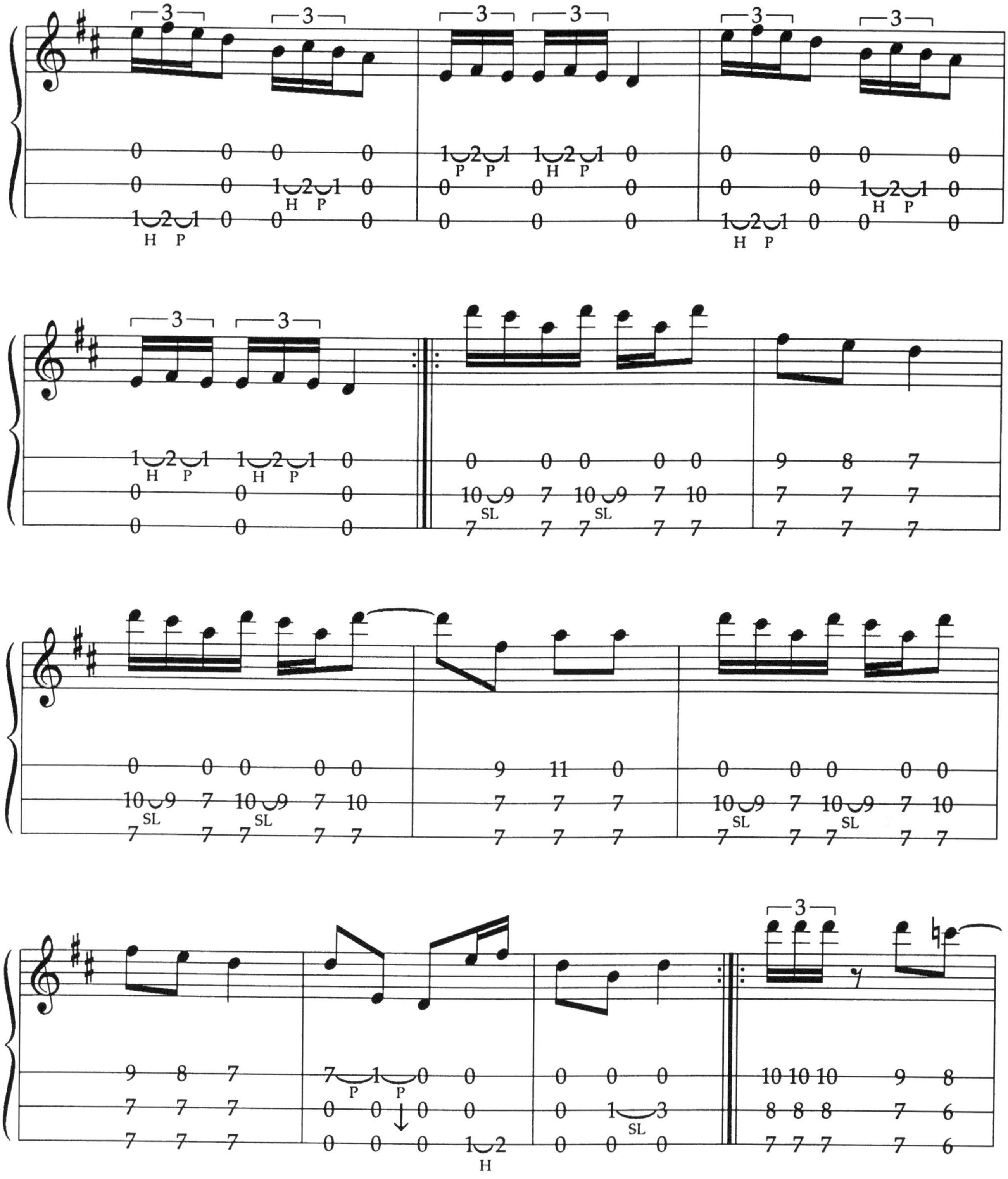

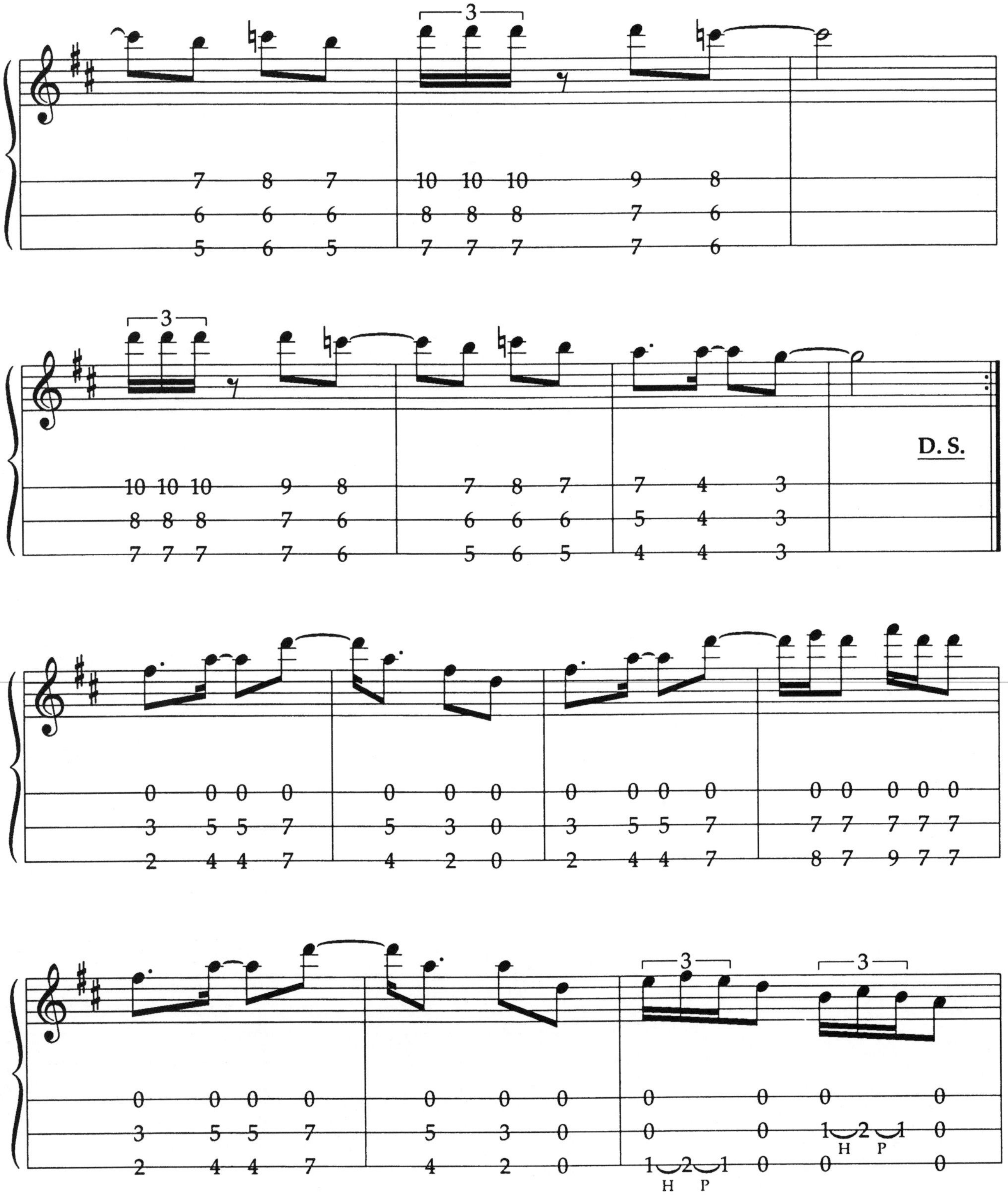
D. S.

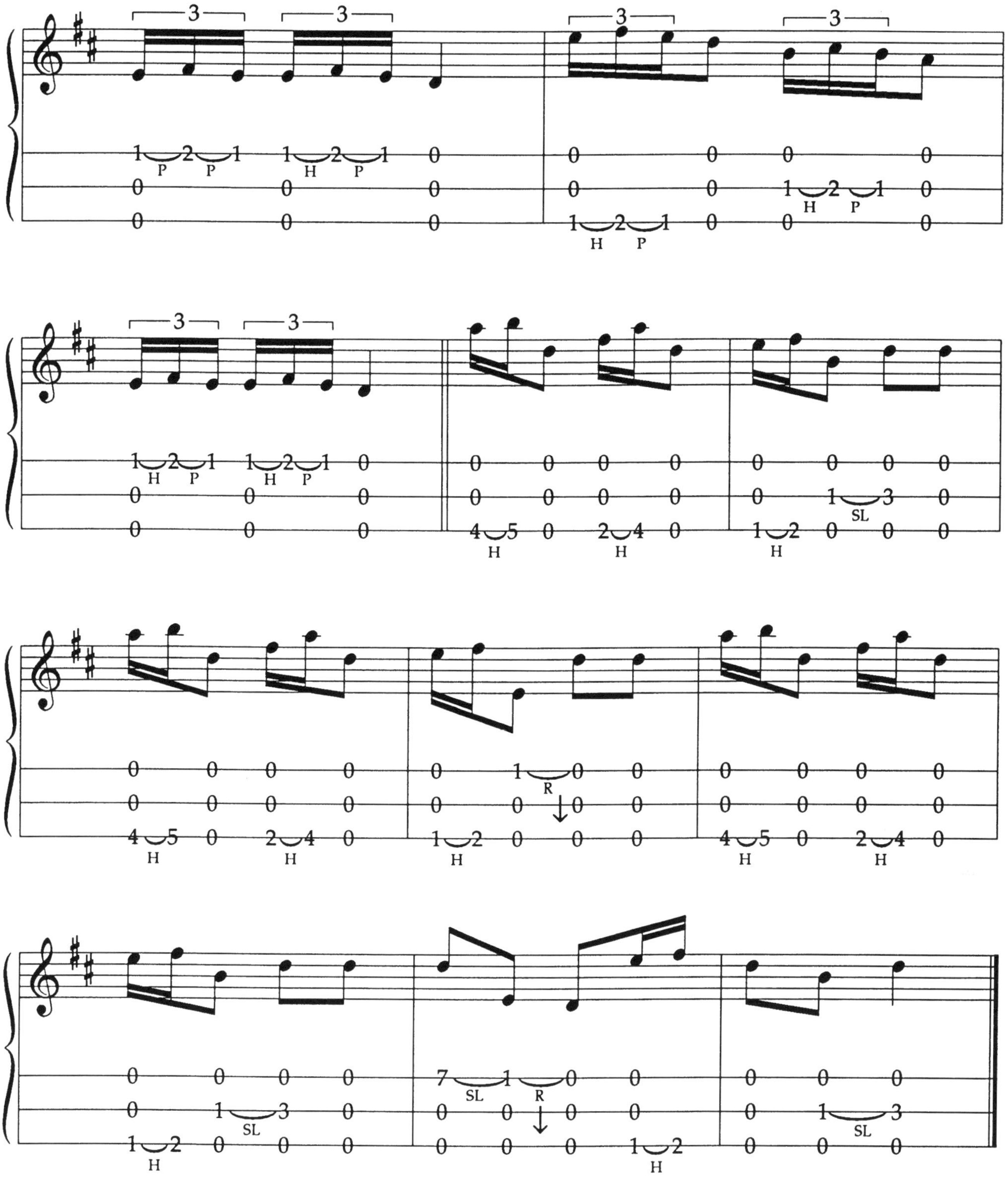

NOW MY DEAR COMPANIONS

Tune : DD-A-D

Shaker Hymn

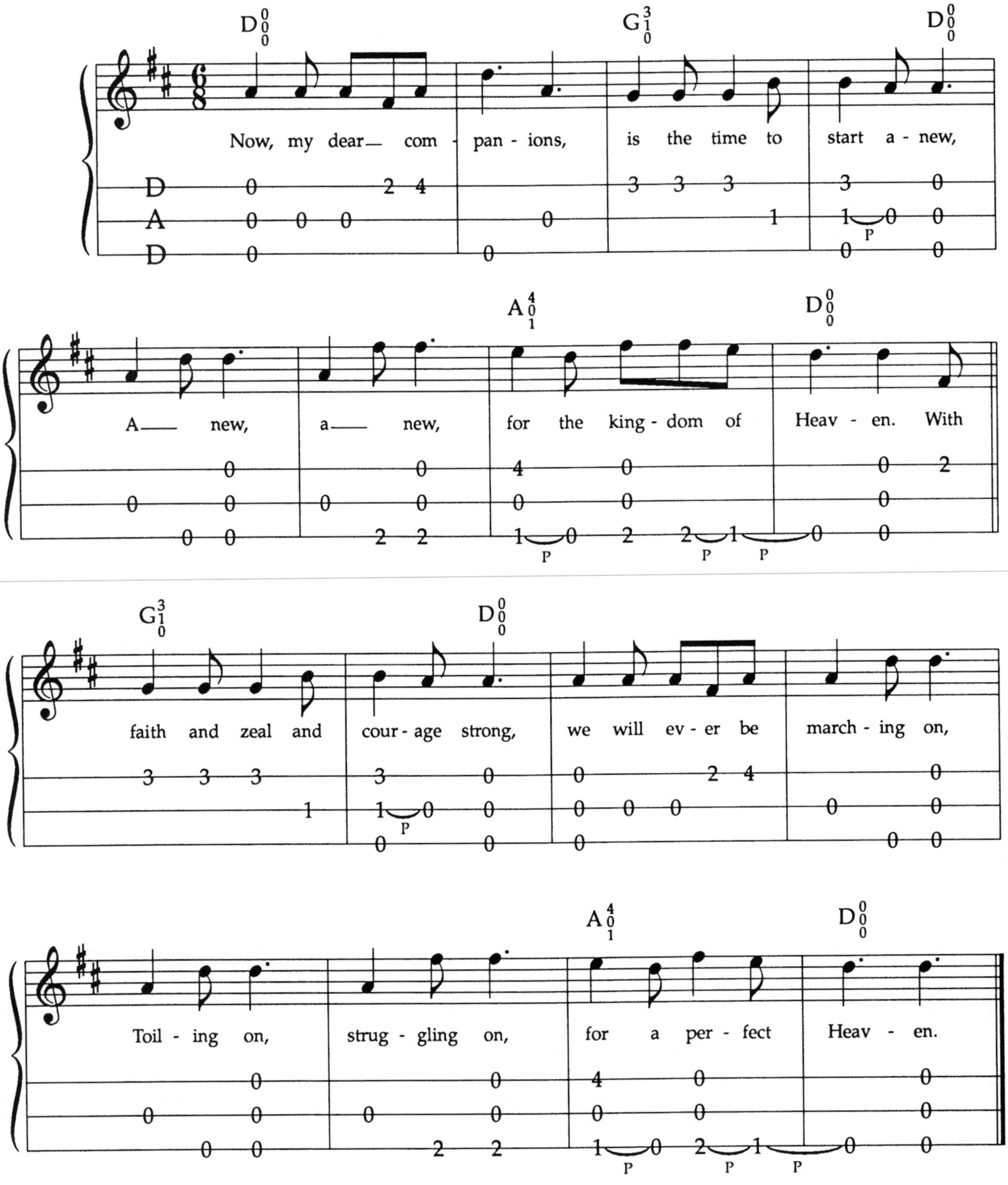

PAVANE FOR A SLEEPING BEAUTY

Tune : DD-A-D

Maurice Ravel
(1875-1937)

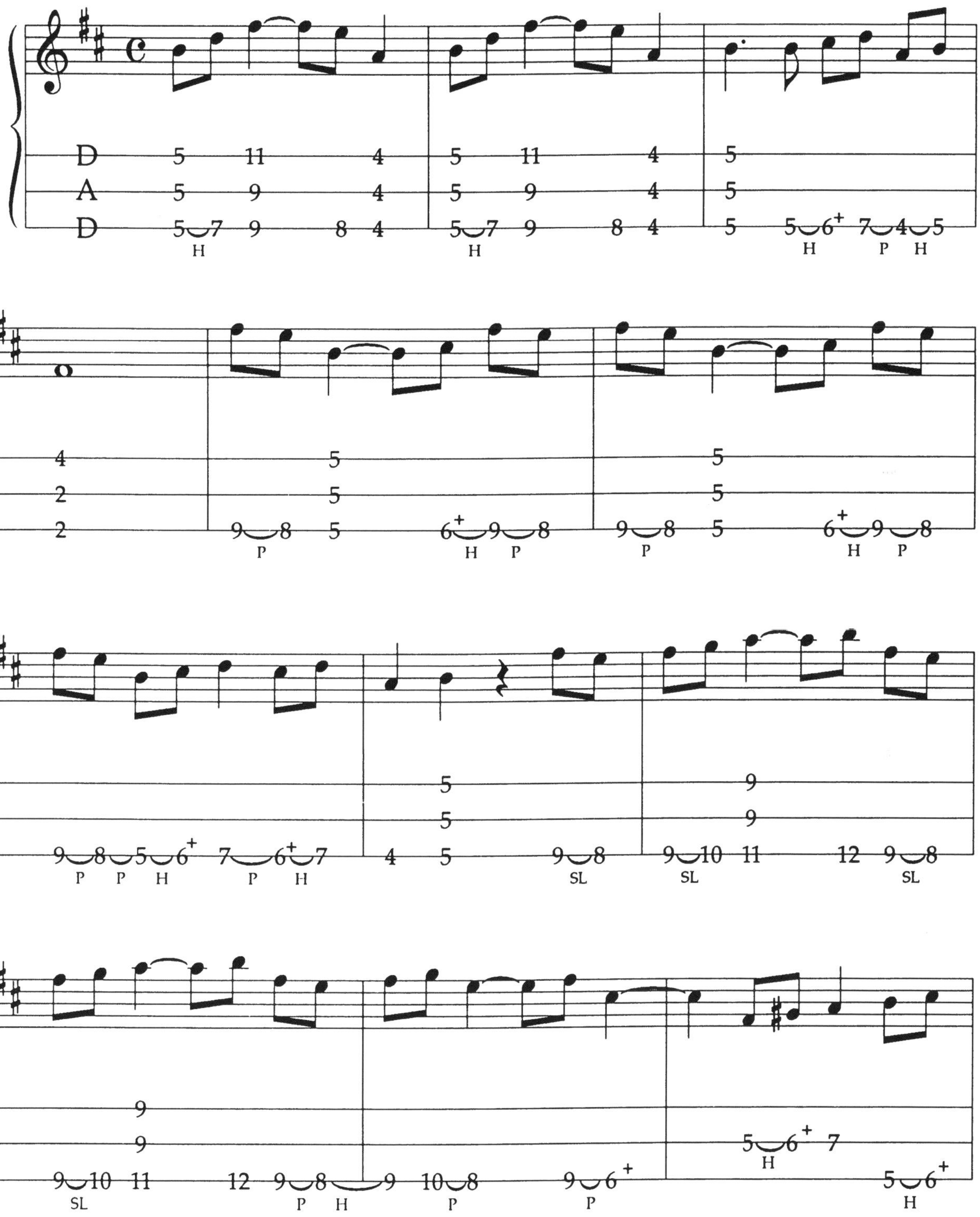

H
H
H
P
H
P
P
H
P
P
H
P
P
P
H
P
H

PICNIC ON THE ST. CROIX

Tune : Eb-Eb-Ab-Eb

Neal Hellman

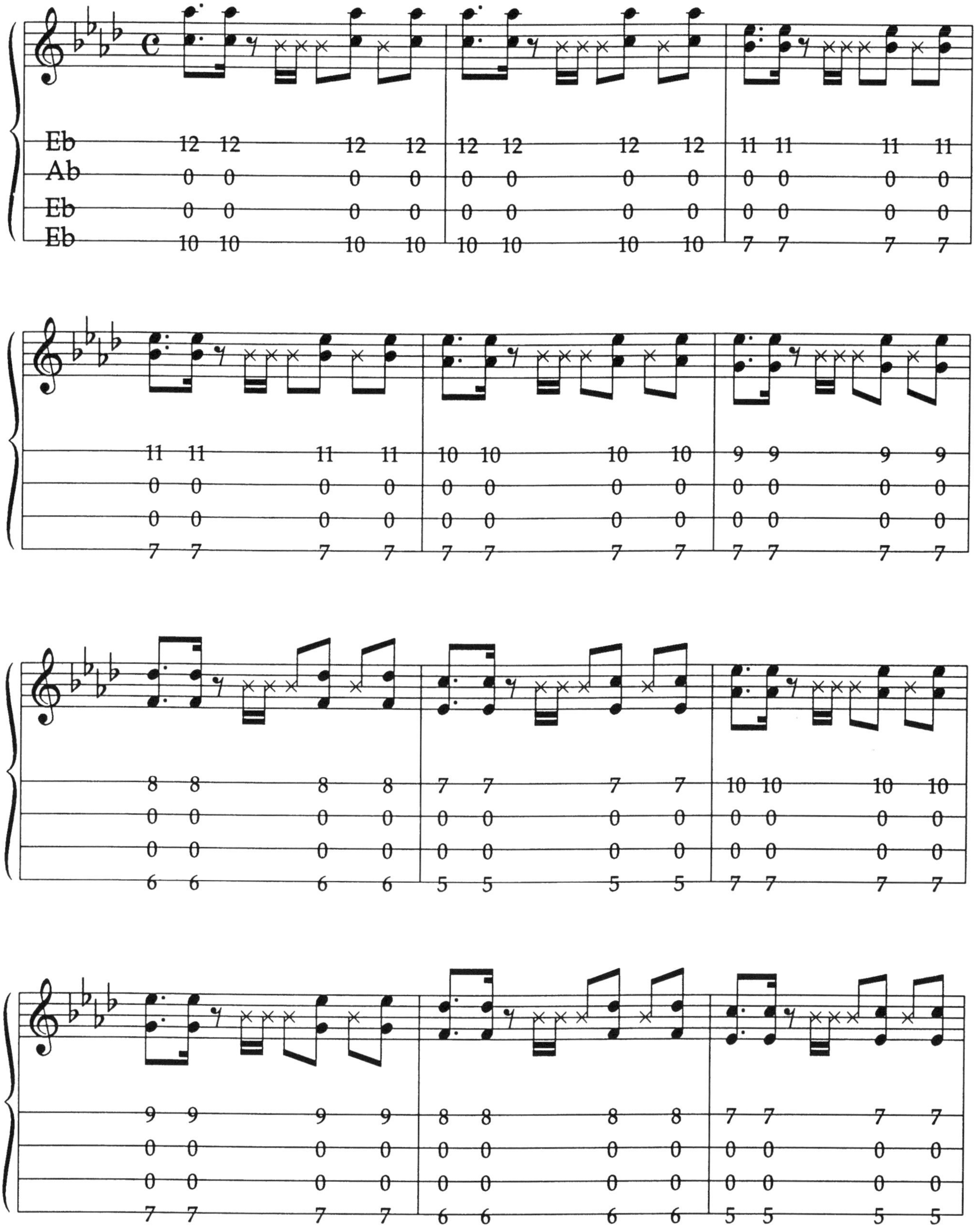

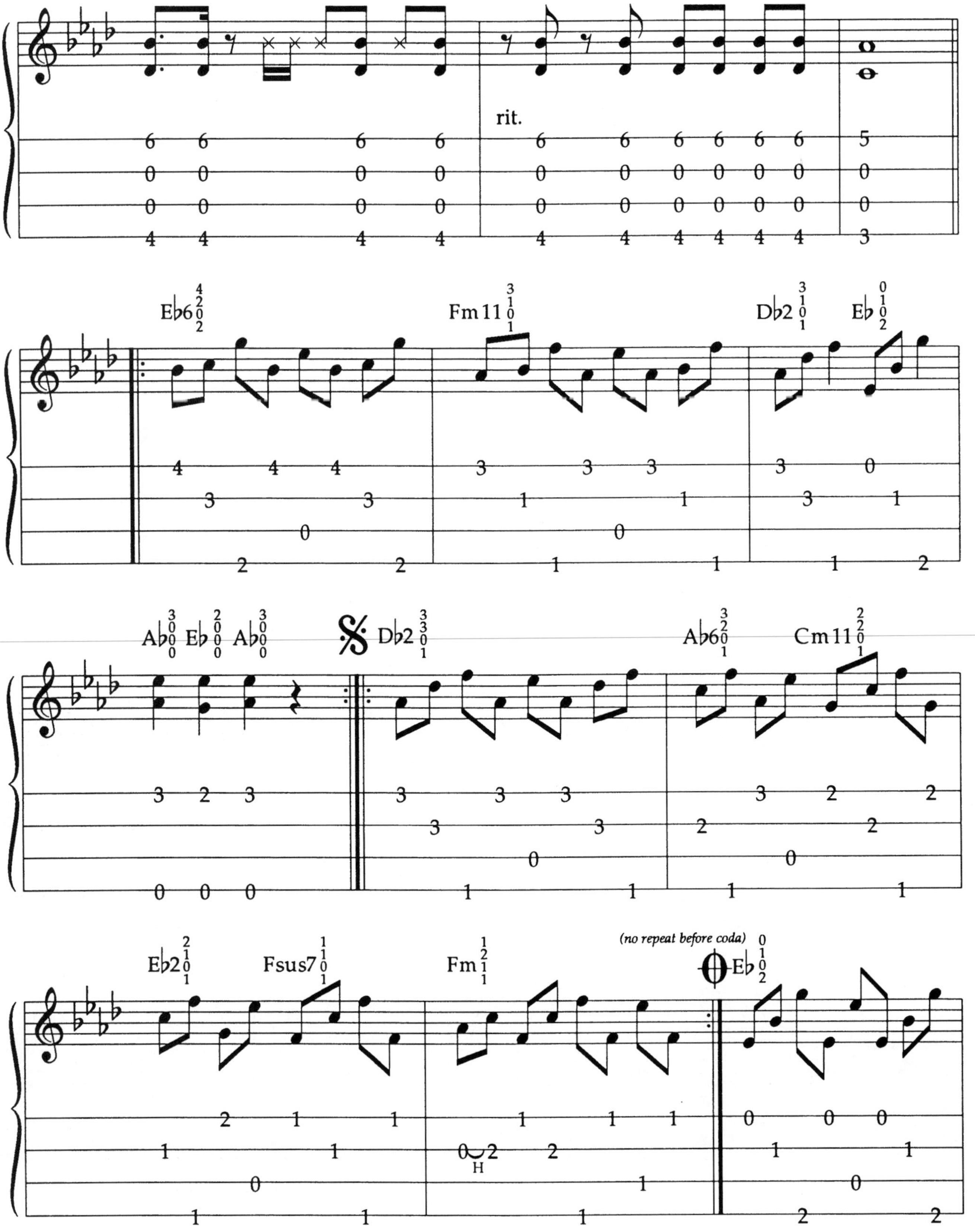
rit.
E♭6
Fm11
D♭2
E♭
A♭
E♭
A♭
D♭2
A♭6
Cm11
E♭2
Fsus7
Fm
(no repeat before coda)
E♭
H

Cm
E♭
rit.
1,3

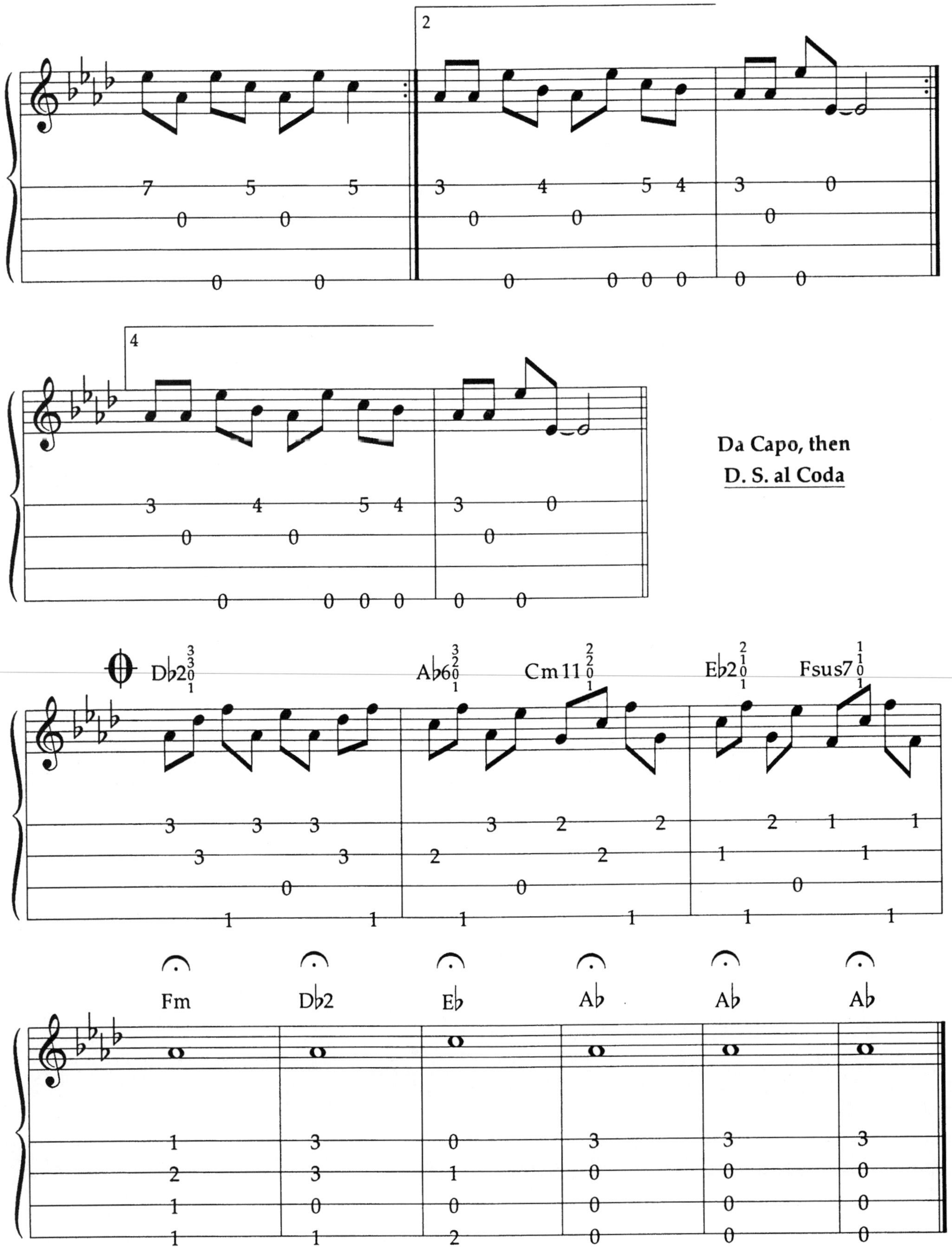
Da Capo, then
D. S. al Coda
D♭2
A♭6
Cm11
E♭2
Fsus7
Fm
D♭2
E♭
A♭
A♭
A♭

PLANXTY ELEANOR PLUNKETT

Tune : DD-A-D

Turlough O'Carolan
(1670-1738)

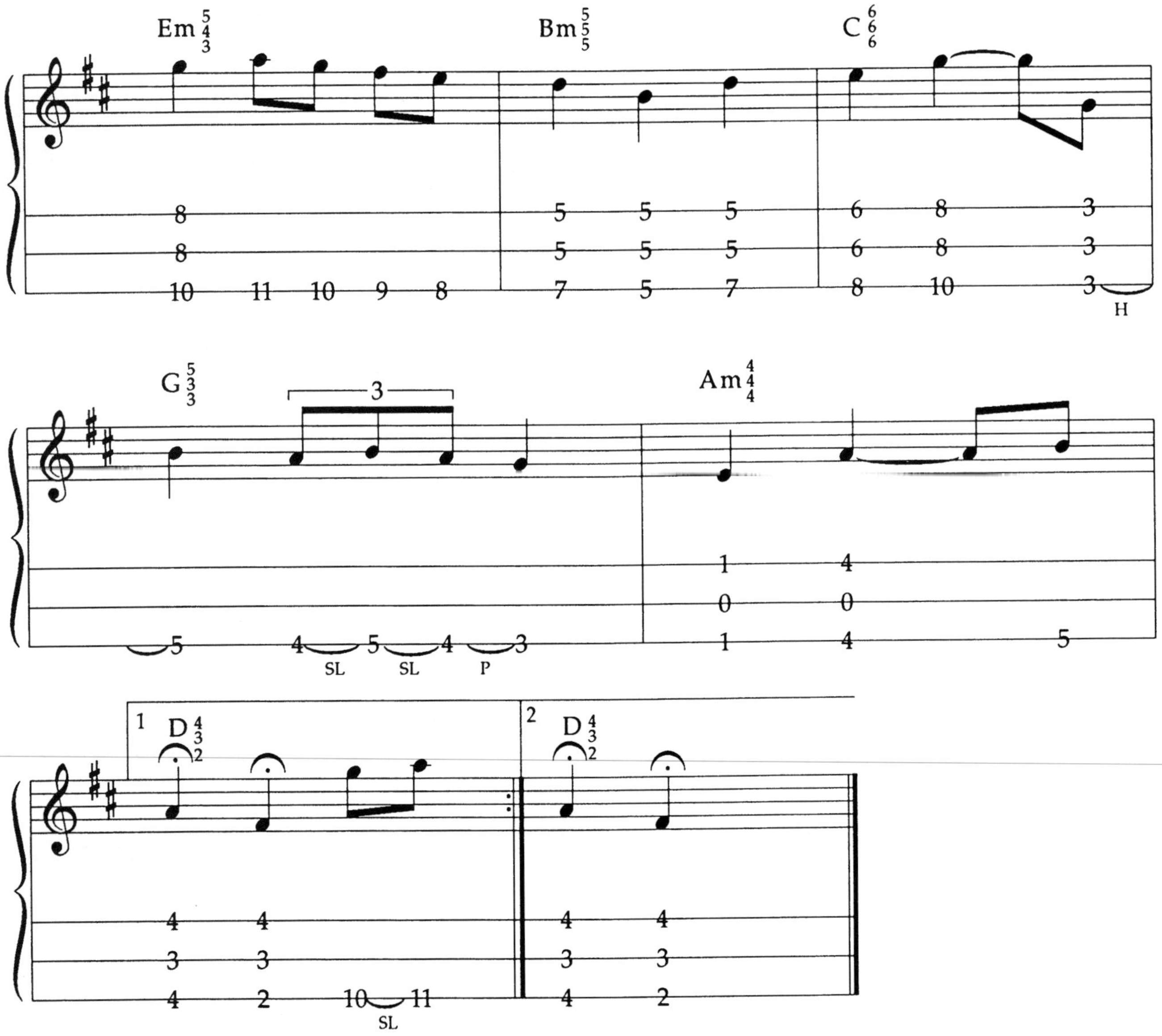
Em
Bm
C
H
G
SL
SL
P
Am
1
D
SL
2
D

PLANXTY GEORGE BRABAZON

Tune : DD-A-D

Turlough O'Carolan
(1670-1738)

Em
A
D
A
D
G
A
1
D
2
D

THE ROAD TO LISDOONVARNA

Tune : DD-A-D

Traditional Irish

ROBERTSON'S UNREEL

Tune : DD-A-D

Neal Hellman

Bm
Em
F♯
Bm
A
Em
Em
Bm
A
Em
D. C. al Fine

RONDEAU

Tune : DD-A-D

Jean Mouret
(1682-1738)

P
H
P
P
P
P
H
P
P
H
P
H
P
H
P
P
P
P
P
SL
SL
P
P
H
H
SL
H
P
H

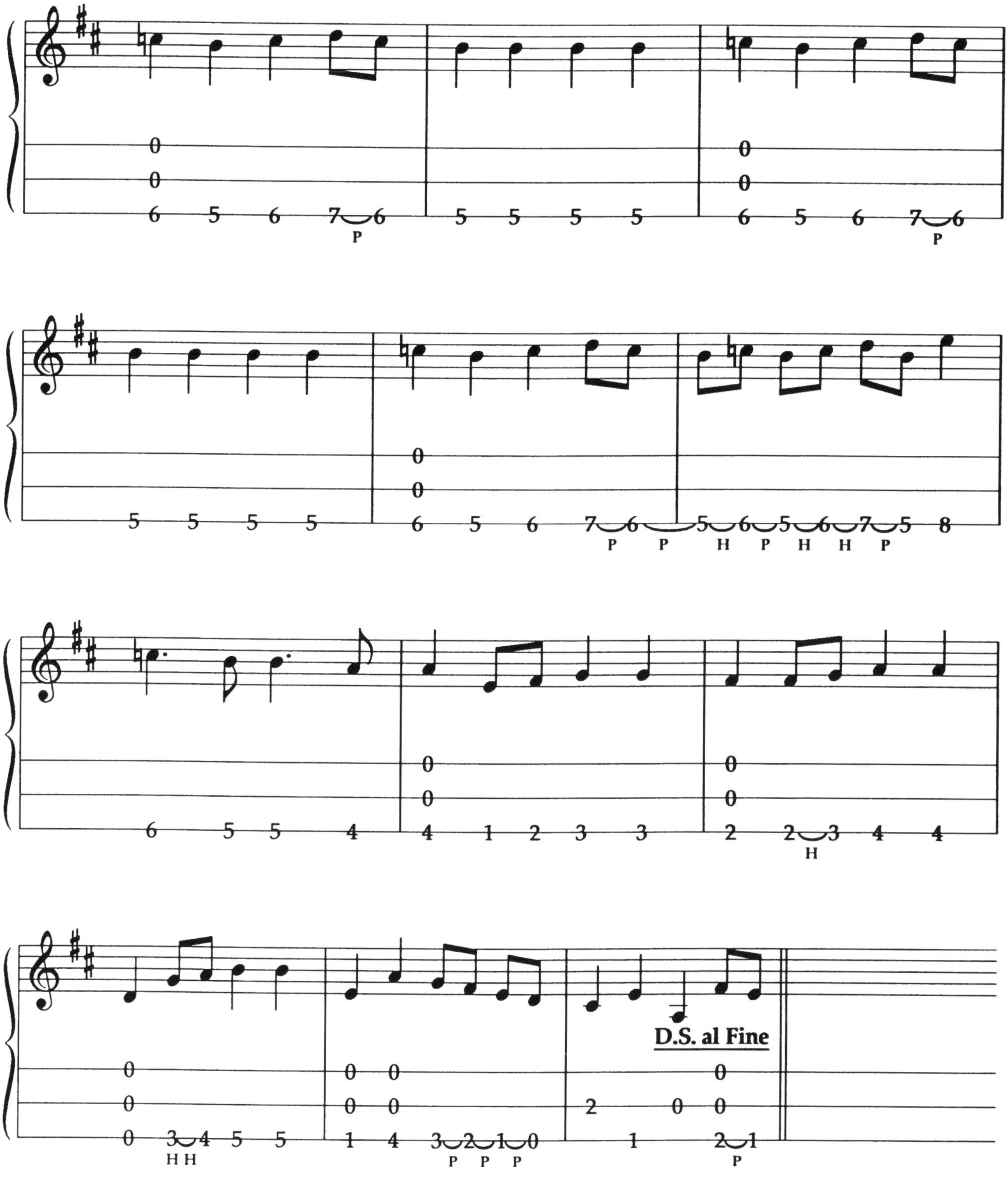
D.S. al Fine

THE SAILOR'S ALPHABET

Tune : DD-A-D

Traditional

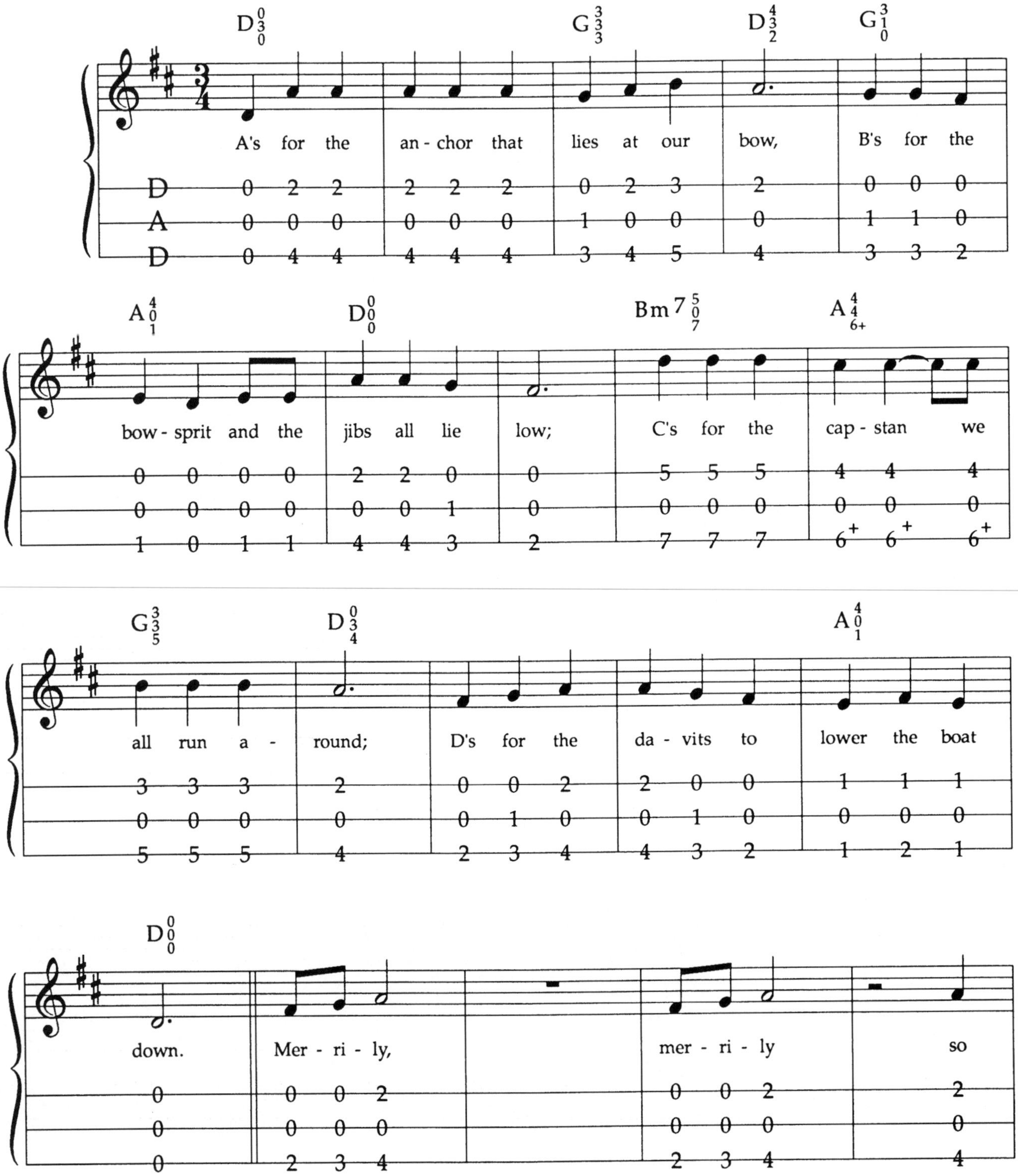

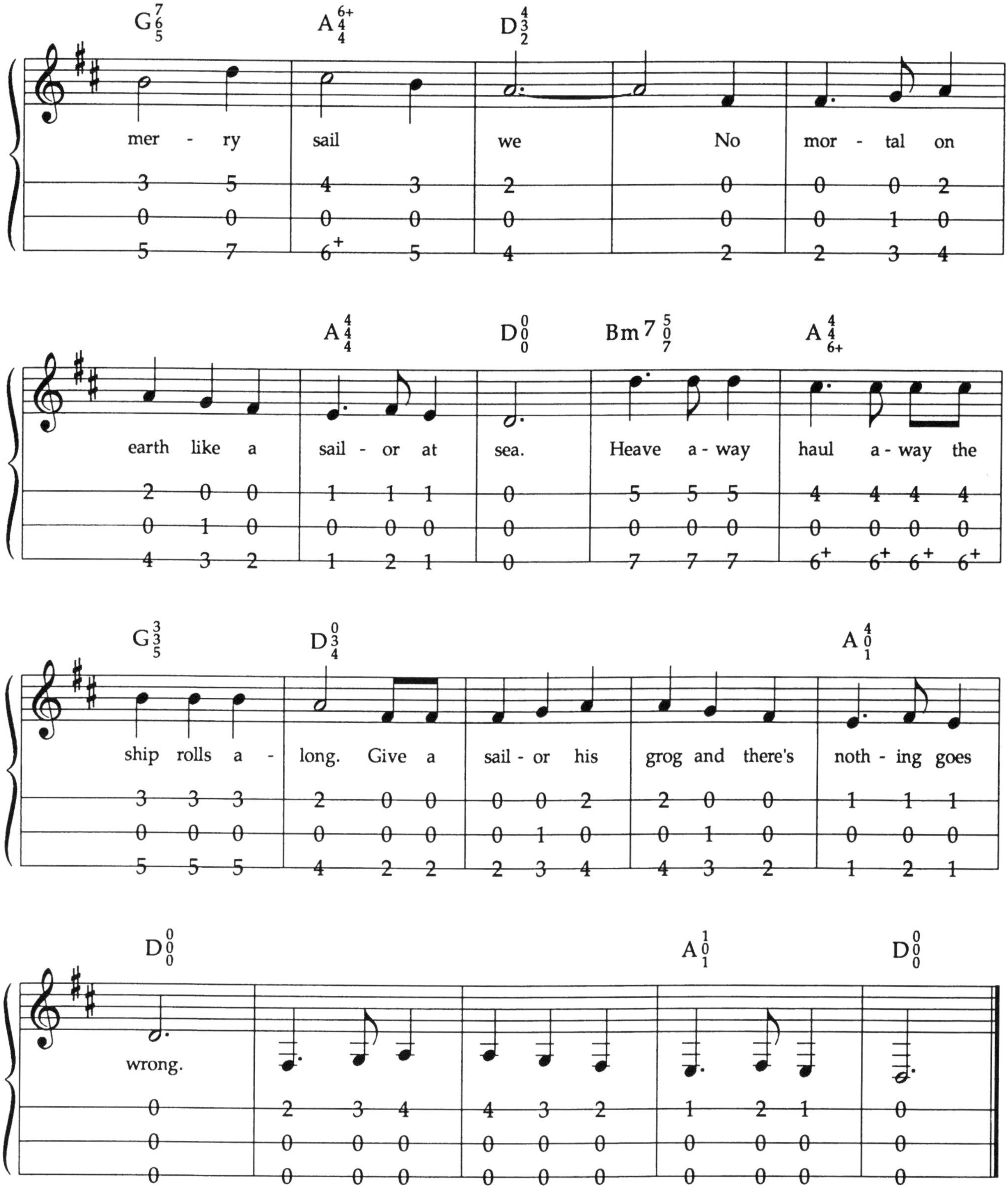
G A D
mer - ry sail we No mor - tal on
A D Bm7 A
earth like a sail - or at sea. Heave a - way haul a - way the
G D A
ship rolls a - long. Give a sail - or his grog and there's noth - ing goes
D A D
wrong.

E's for the ensign that at our peak flew
F's for the foc'sle where lives our wild crew
G's for the galley where the salt junk smells strong
H is for the halyards we hoist with a song.

I's for the eyebolt no good for the feet
J's for the jib, boys, stand by the main sheet
K's for the knightheads where the petty officer stands
L's for the leeside hard found by new hands.

Chorus

M's for the mainmast, it's stout and it's strong
N's for the needle that never points wrong
O's for the oars of our jolly old boat
P's for the pinnace that lively do float.

Q's for the quarterdeck where our officers stand
R's for the rudder that keeps the ship in command
S's for the stunsails that drive her along
T's for the topsail, to get there takes long.

Chorus

U's for the uniform mostly worn aft
V's for the vangs running from the main shaft
W's for the water we're a pint and a pound
X marks the spot where old Salty was drowned.

Y's for the yardarm needs a good sailorman
Z's for the Zoe, I'm her fancy man
Z's also for zero in the cold wintertime
And now we have brought all the letters in rhyme.

Chorus

SHEEBEG AND SHEEMORE

Tune : DD-A-D

Turlough O'Carolan
1670-1738

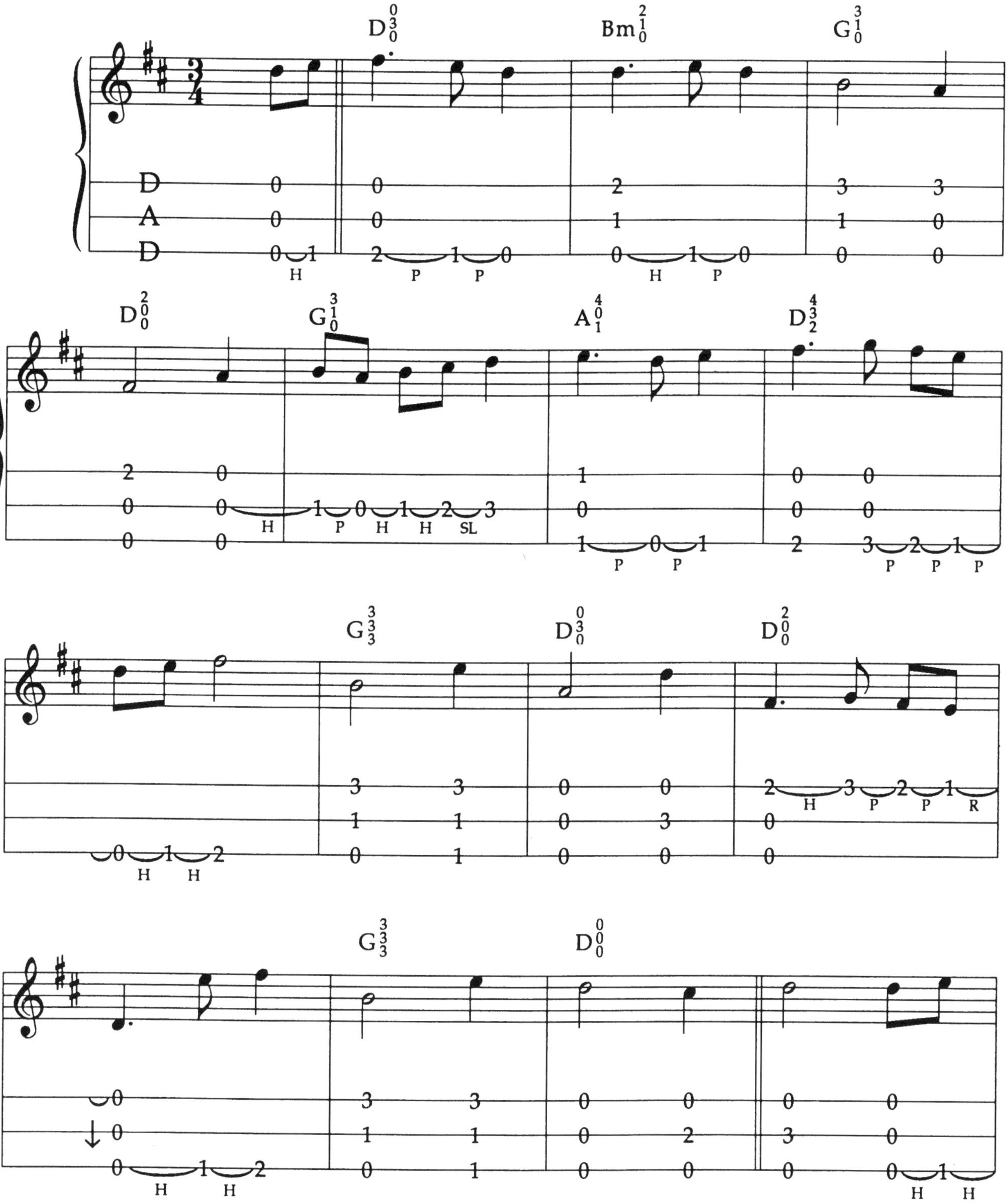

Bm G D
A D G
D G D
G Em A D G D

SPAGNOLETTA

Tune : DD-A-D

Michael Praetorius
1569-1621

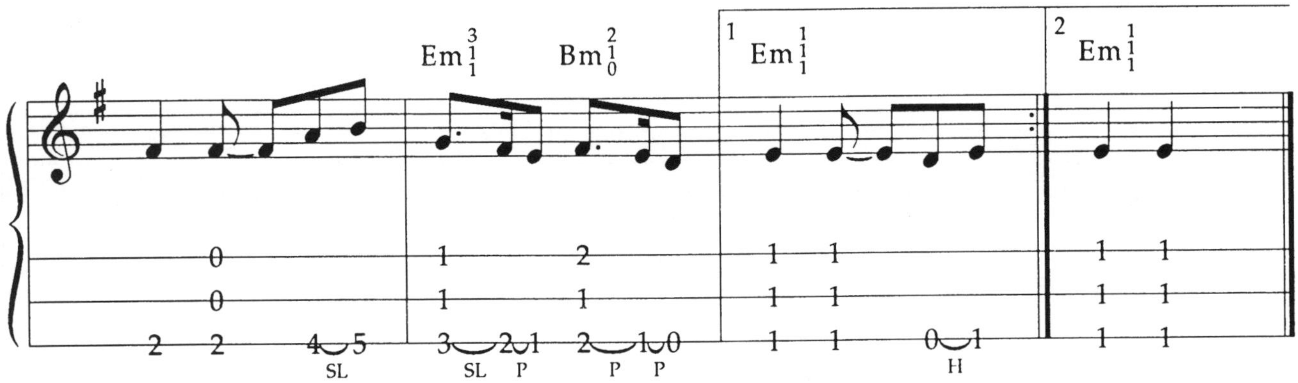
Em
Bm
Em
Em
SL
SL P
P P
H

YOUNG WILLIAM PLUNKETT

Tune : DD-A-D

Turlough O'Carolan
(1670-1738)

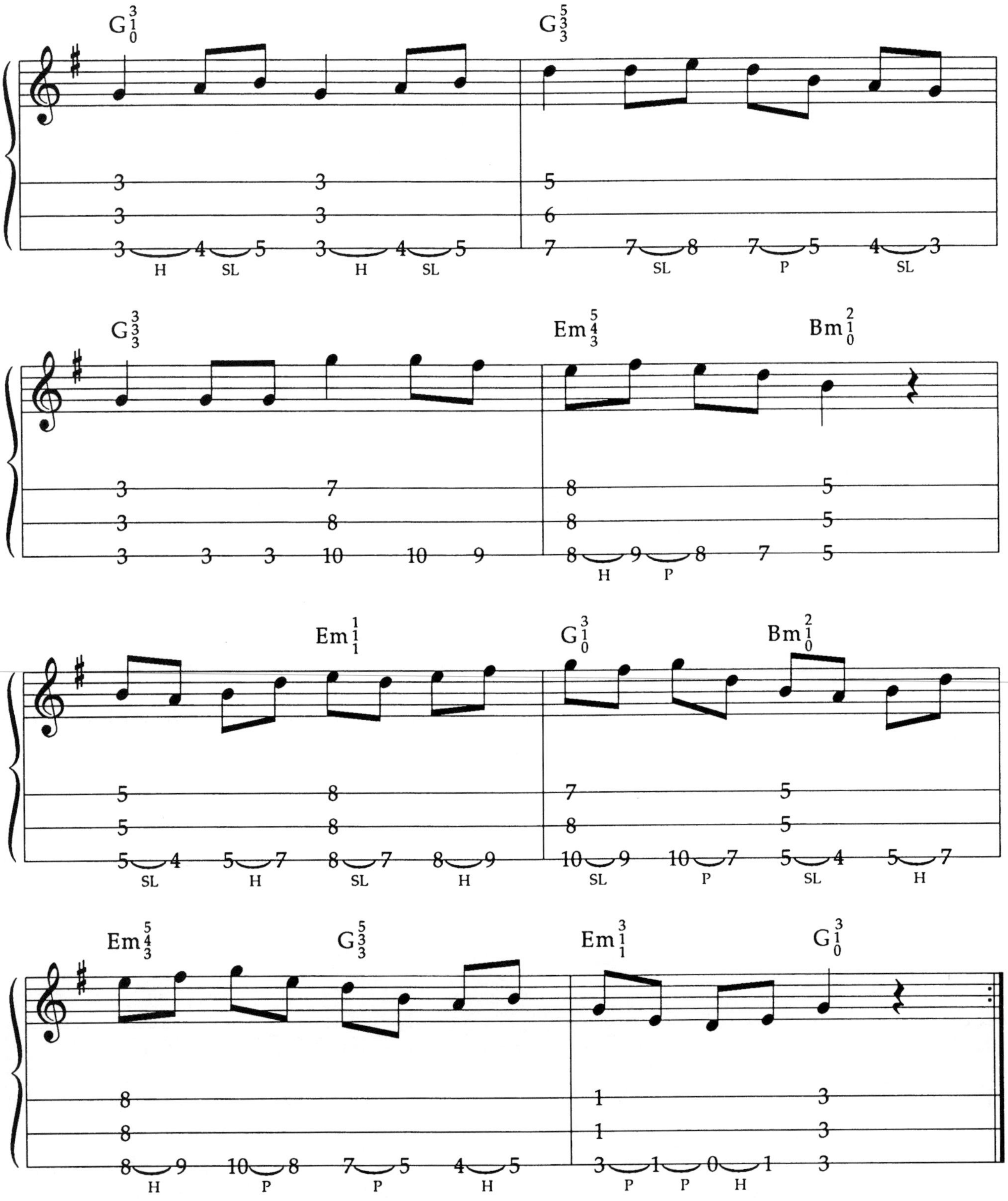
G
G
H SL H SL
SL P SL
G
Em
Bm
H P
Em
G
Bm
SL H SL H
SL P SL H
Em
G
Em
G
H P P H
P P H

Tune :

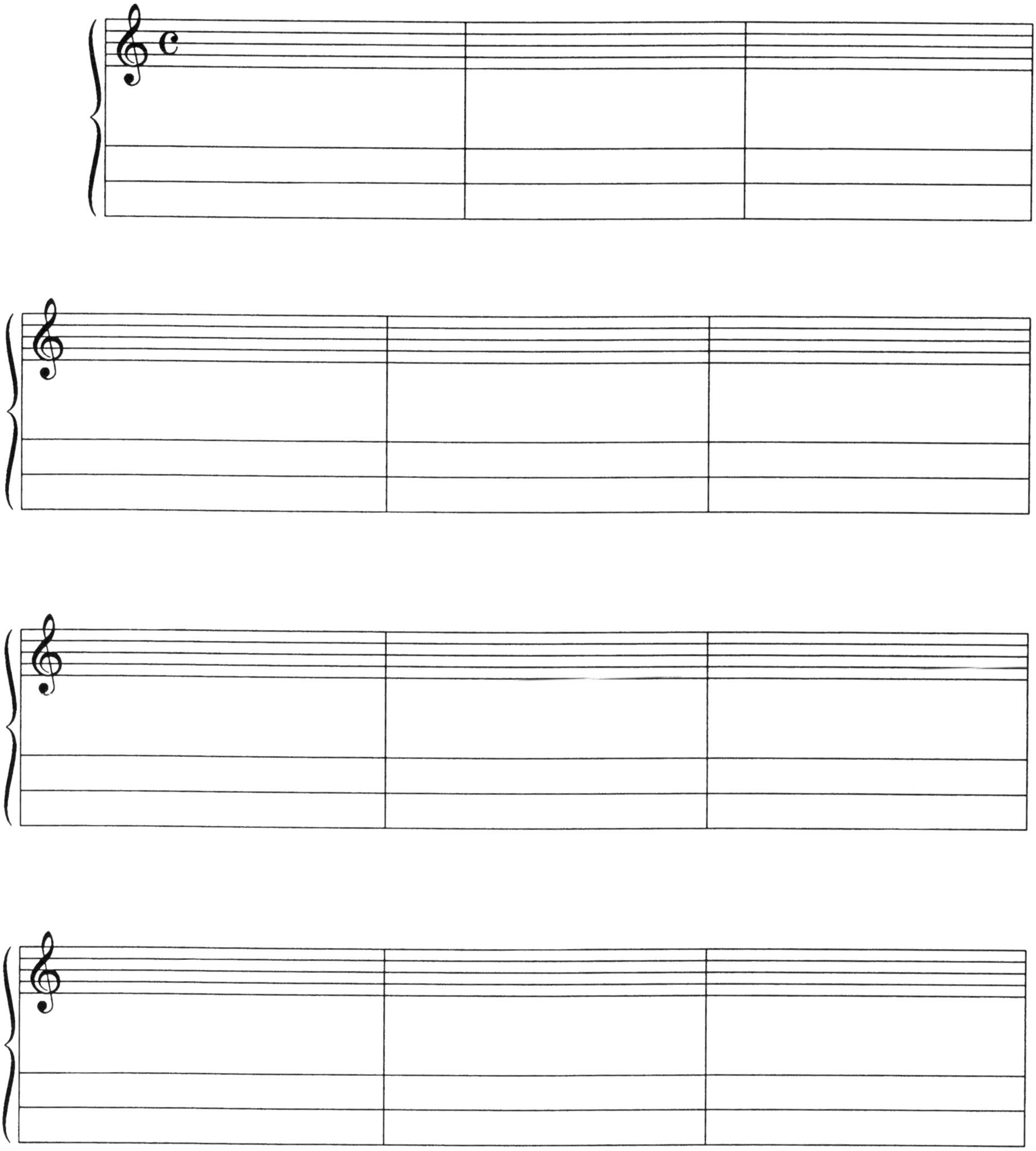

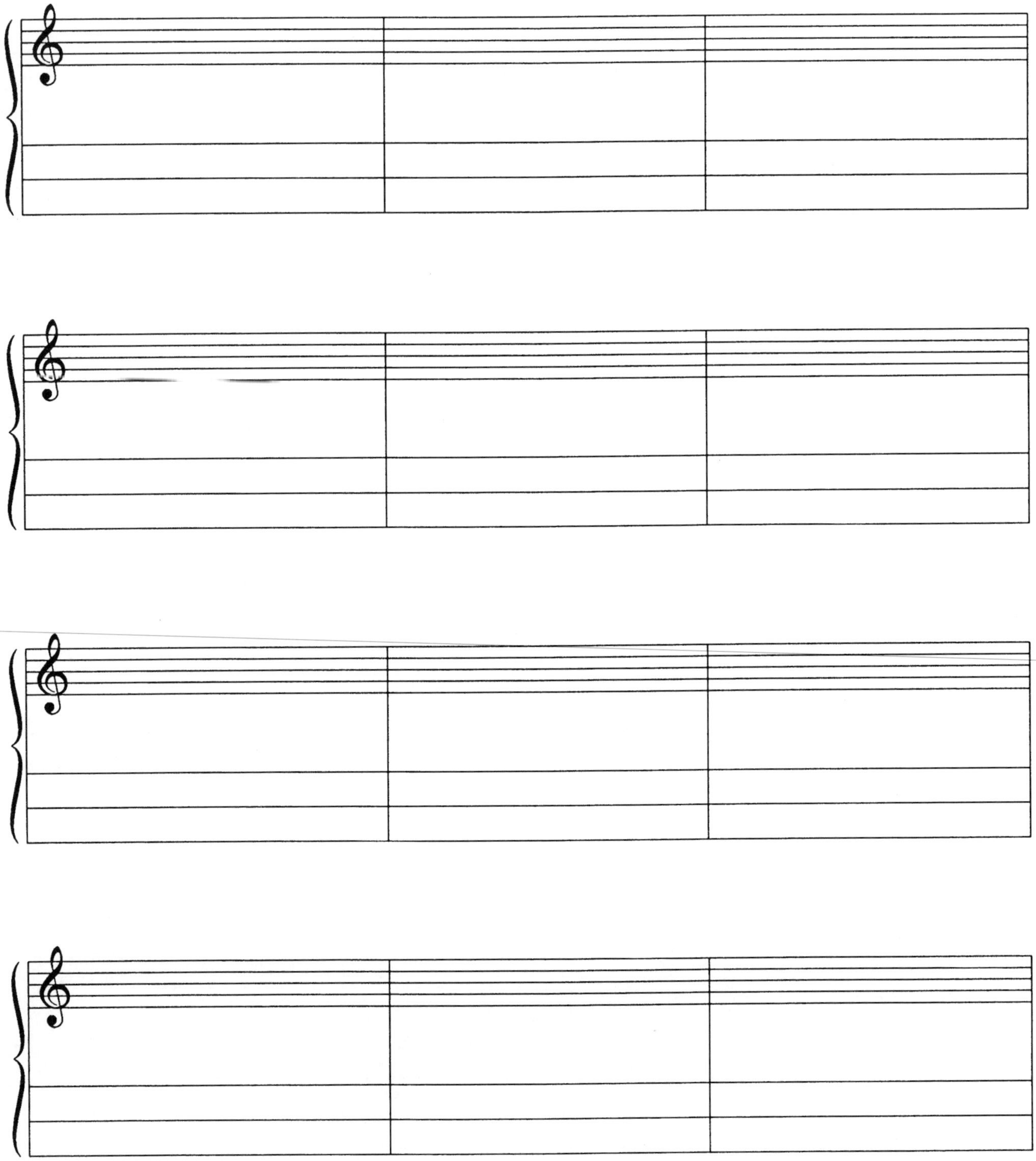

10070698R0008

Made in the USA
Charleston, SC
04 November 2011